Active Learning and Active Citizenship:

Theoretical Contexts

Edited by

Mike McManus and Gary Taylor

Published 2009

© Sociology, Anthropology, Politics (C-SAP),
The Higher Education Academy Network

University of Birmingham
Birmingham, B15 2TT

E-mail: enquiries@c-sap.bham.ac.uk

Website: http://www.c-sap.bham.ac.uk
© 2009 selection and editorial matter, the Higher Education Academy;
individual chapters, the contributors

ISBN 1 902191 38 2

C-SAP Monographs

Monograph No. 1: Benchmarking and Quality Management: The debate in UK Higher Education. Edited by David Jary

Monograph No. 2: Teaching Rites and Wrongs: Universities and the Making of Anthropologists. Edited by David Mills and Mark Harris

Monograph No. 3: Perspectives and Practice in Widening Participation in the Social Sciences. Edited by David Jary and Rob Jones

Monograph No. 4: Engagements with Learning and Teaching in Higher Education. Edited by Denise Carter and Michaela Lord

Monograph No. 5: Teaching Race in the Social Sciences. Edited by Malcolm Todd and Max Farrar

Monograph No. 6: Reflections on Practice: Teaching 'Race' & Ethnicity in Further and Higher Education. Edited by Malcolm Todd and Steve Spencer

Monograph No. 7: Pedagogies of Teaching 'Race' and Ethnicity in Higher Education - British and European Experiences. Edited by Susie Jacobs

Monograph No. 8: Learning and Teaching Social Theory. Edited by Jon Cope, Joyce Canaan and Dave Harris

Monograph No. 9: Teaching Race in Social Science and Humanities Higher Education. Edited by Emily Horowitz

Monograph No. 10: Active Learning and Active Citizenship: Theoretical Concepts. Edited by Mike McManus and Gary Taylor

Contents

Contributors

Hugh Bochel is Professor of Public Policy, University of Lincoln. Recent publications include *Social Policy: Issues and Developments* (with Catherine Bochel, Robert Page and Rob Sykes) (2005), *Welfare Policy* under *New Labour: Views from Inside Westminster* (with Andrew Defty) (2007) and *Making Policy in Theory and Practice* (edited, with Sue Duncan) (2007).

Patrick Dillon has degrees in biological science, economic history and education. He is Professor of Education at the University of Joensuu, Finland and Emeritus Professor at the University of Exeter. He has worked in higher education for twenty-eight years and before that he worked in industry and taught in primary and secondary schools. He has cross-disciplinary interests in culture, education and technology that encompass cultural heritage education, creativity, design education and e-learning. He also researchers and writes on landscape and environmental education out of which has emerged his belief in the value of integrating ecological perspectives into theories of education.

Karl Donert is a National Teaching Fellow of the Higher Education Academy and Director of Development at Liverpool Hope University. He is a geographer with interests in the development of ICT in learning and teaching and the establishment of responsible autonomous learners. He is coordinator of the HERODOT thematic network for Geography in higher education (www.herodot.net) and President of EUROGEO (the European Network of Geography Teacher Associations). Karl has acted as external evaluator to the ALAC project team.

Yee Wah Foo is Senior Lecturer in Political Science, Policy Studies Research. Her research interests include Chinese modern history and inter-allied diplomacy during the Second World War, political theory and the environment.

Janet Kay is a Principal Lecturer in Children and Childhood at Sheffield Hallam University. She is currently completing a Ph.D. entitled 'Parenting in Sibling Adoption'. Recent publications include *Working Together in Children's Services* (with D. Fitzgerald) (2008) and a second edition of *Understanding Early Years Policy* (with P. Baldock and D. Fitzgerald) (2005) (2008). In addition, a chapter on citizenship and early childhood students arising from the ALAC project (by Janet Kay and Caroline Bath) is included in a book of papers from a conference at Anglia Ruskin in 2007 on *Reclaiming Relational Pedagogy* edited by Janet Moyles (2009).

Jo Long is postgraduate tutor at Sheffield Hallam University. She specialises in teaching research methods and study skills and has published on work based learning and the community.

Richard McCarter is a lecturer in e-learning at Sheffield Hallam University specialising in the use of rich media digital learning content and staff development. He has been a television producer since 1986 working in higher education and training organisations. Much of his work concentrated on the value of combining text and video in multimedia work and his interests are now focused on the use of web 2.0 technologies and its impact on learning.

Mike McManus is Senior Lecturer in Social Policy at Sheffield Hallam University. He was the Project Manager for the ALAC project from 2005 to 2008, having previously been involved in numerous educational projects. He has a long-standing interest in pedagogy, stemming from his early teaching days as a lecturer in the philosophy of education and a concern that the pursuit of high-quality teaching should be given an enhanced status in higher education.

Liam Mellor has recently completed his Masters in Political Communication at the University of Sheffield and is currently working with Gary Taylor on a range of projects on the politics of the media and on work-based learning.

Gary Saunders joined the University of Lincoln in 2007 as a research assistant in the Department of Policy Studies and now works as Research Officer in the Centre for Educational and Research Development at the University. He studied as an undergraduate at the University of Lincoln and as a postgraduate at Nottingham Trent University where he gained his degree in law and criminology and an M.Sc. in social research methods respectively. Gary has worked on numerous pedagogical research projects in the areas of action learning, collaborative learning, learning space, online learning and assessment feedback. In addition, Gary teaches on the undergraduate criminology programme and the postgraduate globalising justice Masters degree and is currently studying for his PGDE at the University of Lincoln.

Gary Taylor is Principal Lecturer in Applied Social Science at Sheffield Hallam University. His teaching interests include social and political theory, the media and work-based learning. His recent publications include *Ideology and Welfare* (2007), *Social Identities* (edited, with S. Spencer) and *Democracy and Participation* (edited, with M. Todd). He is currently co-authoring book on health policy for Open University Press.

Lizzie Walton is postgraduate student at Sheffield Hallam University. She is currently working on a CSAP project on the experiences of students with disabilities.

Part I: Active Learning

Chapter 1

Introduction

Mike McManus and Gary Taylor

What does it mean to be a good citizen? How do we learn about our social and political environments? Are active citizens also active learners? These were the type of questions the authors of this monograph considered in the early stages of their HEFCE project on active learning and active citizenship (ALAC) and the issues we continue to debate in this monograph. Our intention is to provide a theoretical framework that can be used to discuss active learning, active citizenship and the relationship between the two. It is our belief that this taps into two important agendas. In terms of pedagogy, we are urged to move away from 'chalk and talk' methods and to embrace more participative, adaptive and lively approaches to our teaching. The authors contained herein share a commitment to the development of autonomous and active learners. But we also live in a political climate where the State has withdrawn from some areas of economic, social and cultural life. Instead of being passive recipients of what the State has to offer or defenceless victims of the free market, we are urged to take greater responsibility for ourselves and for the welfare of our communities. The idea of active citizenship has become increasingly evident in political discourse, and, whilst we might have some reservations about the ways in which this agenda is pursued, the vision of a society of active citizens is still appealing. A shared interest and commitment to active learning and active citizenship has prompted us to write this monograph and to explore these concepts in a variety of ways. Let us start by addressing these ideas in the abstract.

Active Learning

There is no universally accepted definition of 'active learning'; indeed, some would say that all learning is active by definition as it is normally thought of as an activity, as something a person does. Could there be such a thing as 'inactive learning'? How could someone learn by not doing anything? Is there any validity in the 'osmosis' method of learning as favoured by some students, where just sitting in the library enables them to learn by ingesting all the knowledge contained in the books? Sadly, we know that this does not work. Sometimes people say that they just 'picked it up'. For example, someone might say that they never formally learnt how to cook: they just picked it up by trying things out or by watching someone else cook. In this case though, they will have acquired the knowledge or skill by paying attention to what was being done in front of them or they will have acquired the skill through repetition and trial and error. Quite often these statements refer to the fact that they did not undergo formal teaching in order to acquire the knowledge or skill and highlight the point that there is no necessary connection between learning and teaching. There can be learning with no teaching, and, equally, there can be teaching with no learning. It is this latter point that has led some academics to argue for 'active learning' (Felder and Brent 2003; Fink 1999; Prince 2004).

What 'active learning' generally refers to is a method of instruction that involves the active engagement of students in the learning process. This requires more than the traditional taking of notes from a lecture session or the completion of essays outside the formal timetabled sessions. The core elements of active learning are student activity, student engagement, student reflection and the use of higher-order academic skills such as analysis, synthesis and evaluation. It has been identified in the National Framework for Active Learning for Active Citizenship (Communities and Local Government [CLG] 2006) as an important element in the development of citizenship among students. This is because it is viewed a flexible approach that involves 'experiential learning' in group settings which are characterised by 'the values of participation, co-operation, social justice and equality with diversity. These values require the work to be: (i) community based, (ii) learner centred, and (iii) developed through active and reflective learning' (CLG 2006: 7).

The term 'active learning' is used to describe a range of pedagogic approaches from the simple asking of questions in a class through highly structured problem-based learning exercises and simulations to practical experiential learning in the community outside the educational institution. It might be helpful to briefly discuss some of these approaches before looking in more depth at the theoretical justification for active learning.

Collaborative and Cooperative Learning

There is an extensive literature on the subject of cooperative and collaborative learning, and there is evidence of some confusion over the terms. Panitz (1996: 1) suggests that 'Collaboration is a philosophy of interaction and personal lifestyle whereas cooperation is a structure of interaction designed to facilitate the accomplishment of an end product or goal.' However, an article on collaborative and co-operative learning on another educational website defines the terms in the following way:

> Collaborative learning is a method of teaching and learning in which students team together to explore a significant question or create a meaningful project. A group of students discussing a lecture or students from different schools working together over the Internet on a shared assignment are both examples of collaborative learning.
>
> Cooperative learning [. . .] is a specific kind of collaborative learning. In cooperative learning,

11

students work together in small groups on a structured activity. They are individually accountable for their work, and the work of the group as a whole is also assessed. Cooperative groups work face to face and learn to work as a team.

(http://www.thirteen.org/edonline/concept2class/coopcollab/index.html)

Panitz seems concerned to separate the two terms rather than regard one as a subset of the other. On the other hand, Johnson et al. state that 'Cooperative learning is a generic term referring to numerous methods for organising and conducting classroom teaching' (2000: 4). To add to the potential confusion, the term 'cooperative education' is used outside the UK to refer to work-based learning such as that experienced in placement years of degrees. The Canadian Association For Cooperative Education (CAFCE): 'Co-operative Education is a program that formally integrates a student's academic studies with work experience with participating employers' (CAFCE 2005: 1).

What seems to be at issue here is whether we are talking about a methodology or whether we are talking about a theoretical pedagogic position which encapsulates a number of basic values, such as student empowerment, the power, role and status of teachers, and the nature of knowledge. In essence, do we regard the curriculum as a transactional or a transformational process?

Problem-Based Learning

Problem-based learning (PBL) is another generic term that includes inquiry- based learning (IBL), enquiry-based learning (EBL) and problem-solving learning (PSL). PBL is mostly associated with the development of medical education in North America and engineering education in Canada at McMaster University. PBL in its initial form was a highly structured approach, but it has now become such a popular and common concept in education that it is used to describe a range of educational practices that the original inventors of problem based learning would not include in their definition (Barrows 2007). The essence of the approach is to arrange teaching material around case studies or scenarios rather than a particular academic discipline, with the aim of enabling learners to engage with a self-determined process of enquiry. In medical education, the aim is to assist with the correct identification of a specific patient's symptoms, and, for that reason, there has been a move to EBL/IBL in the social sciences on the basis that in social sciences problems tend to be more open-ended with no single solution. The EBL approach is favoured since it encourages students to gain the skill of formulating appropriate skills such as critical thinking, formulating questions and working collaboratively.

One important aspect of PBL is the changed role of the teacher. Rather than having the traditional role of the holder of the knowledge whose task is to transmit it to the learners, the role becomes more of a facilitator or coach whose main responsibility is to listen to the learners so that he or she can guide them in their enquiries. This requires a major reorientation for staff who have been accustomed to a traditional didactic approach and can be a significant obstacle in the adoption of this methodology.

Work-Based Learning

There is a long tradition of work-based or work-related learning in the UK ranging from traditional apprenticeships through the sandwich-year placements on some degrees to the clinical placements undertaken by nursing and other health professions. As previously mentioned, the term 'cooperative education' is also sometimes used to describe this approach to learning. In addition to these terms, the term 'service learning' is used in North America to refer to community-based experiences which are linked to academic studies. All of these learning experiences were designed to enable students to learn from their working environment, an approach that found favour with Ron Dearing in the Report of the National Committee of

Inquiry into Higher Education (NCIHE) (1997): 'Recommendation 18: We recommend that all institutions should, over the medium term, identify opportunities to increase the extent to which programmes help students to become familiar with work, and help them to reflect on such experience.'

The recent report on work placements from the Higher Education Academy (Little and Harvey 2006: 61) reported that 'the overwhelming majority of students perceived positive changes in their approaches to study, as a result of the placement experiences. Such changes related both to issues of confidence and motivation to study generally, and to a sense of more active engagement with learning tasks.'

The use of work-related learning to assist in the teaching of citizenship has long been an aim of service learning as practised in North America, and its purpose has been summarised in 'the principle that community service can be connected to classroom learning in such a way that service is more informed by theoretical and conceptual understanding and learning is more informed by the realities of the world' (California State University Stanislaus 2009). It has its roots in the work of John Dewey and the more recent work of Paulo Freire as well as in the writings of Vygotsky and Bruner. Advocates of this activity have seen it as a way of dealing with issues of social and economic justice as well as raising concerns about the structure and purpose of educational institutions in a democratic society. Hence, learning is seen as transformative in both individuals and organisations and not merely transactional. It is an active process not a passive one. The use of such learning approaches in the UK has recently been studied in the UK as part of the ALAC project (Taylor et al. 2006) and is part of the ongoing work of the Crucible Project at the University of Roehampton (www.roehampton.ac.uk/crucible).

There has recently been much interest in the USA in the concept of 'integrative learning', leading to the establishment of a project by the Carnegie Foundation for the Advancement of Learning as part of its wider work on the academy in transition. Huber and Hutchings (2004: 3) state 'to participate responsibly as local citizens, people must also be "citizens of the world," aware of complex interdependencies and able to synthesize learning from a wide array of sources, to learn from experience and to make productive connections between theory and practice.' This is based on the premise that learners are active and the learning process a potentially transformative experience.

Pedagogy and Active Learning

Underlying the arguments for active learning are several basic pedagogical beliefs which have already been mentioned. First, there is a belief in student autonomy in the learning process although often this is vaguely defined but includes an element of empowerment and an attempt to make students accept more responsibility for their own learning. Much of the approach is based on a social-constructionist view of learning and particularly the work of Biggs on constructive alignment. As Biggs (1994) says, 'the teacher's task is not to transmit correct understandings but to help students construct understandings that are more or less acceptable.' In order to achieve this there will need to be significant activity on the part of the learner that involves both actual content and reflection of the learning process.

The second element is the practice of reflection, what Fink (1999) terms 'dialogue with self' in his model of active learning. This is seen as an essential skill that all learners need to acquire if they are to become active learners. The work of Schon (1987) has gained prominence in nursing education where reflective practice is a core element of all courses, but his writings apply to all work-based learning and, it could be argued, to all learning situations. Unless learners reflect on their progress they will not learn to correct their mistakes, and feedback becomes a formulaic activity.

The third basic element is learner engagement, the process by which the learner makes the learning his or her own. Ownership is closely connected to making sense of learning in terms both of the individual world of the student and the wider world in which they live. If education is seen as a transformative activity, then its main aim, as R. S. Peters (1973: 3–4) says, should be concerned with developing knowledge and understanding which is relevant to people's lives, in the sense that it should enable them to grasp how they are placed in the world and to be at a better vantage-point for determining what they and their fellows are to become. It should provide them with a range of activities that give point to life and so come to terms with its seeming pointlessness.

Evidence for Active Learning

Both Felder and Brent (1994) and Prince (2004) have evaluated active learning and have argued that there is support for this approach from a wide variety of sources. However, as with many teaching initiatives, there are problems involved in its evaluation. The variety of definitions of 'active learning' makes it difficult to identify precisely what is being studied, and many studies focus on one particular aspect – such as problem-based learning, for example (Justice et al. 2001). Moreover, since learning and teaching are complex activities, it is difficult to identify simple causal relationships between a teaching input and a learning outcome. As Prince says, 'solid data on how an instructional method impacts on all . . . learning outcomes is often not available, making comprehensive assessment difficult' (2004: 2). Despite these methodological concerns, there seems to be support for all forms of active learning mentioned in the preceding sections although different methods of active learning may produce different outcomes. Thus, Prince states that active engagement of engineering students produces substantial improvements in recall of information and overall engagement with the course and the subject area. Collaborative approaches seem to enhance academic achievement as well as student attitudes and retention. Similarly, cooperative education has a large role in improving the interpersonal skills of students as well as their academic performance. The evidence for PBL is more mixed, with some suggestions that it may lead to less coverage of factual knowledge but improved skills relating to the formulation of academic questions, the solving of problems and development of life-long learning skills, together with a deeper approach to learning. Prince concludes his article by saying: 'Teaching cannot be reduced to formulaic methods and active learning is not a cure for all educational problems. However, there is broad support for the elements of active learning most commonly discussed in the educational literature and analysed here. Some of the findings are surprising and deserve special attention' (2004: 7).

The ALAC Project and Active Learning

Early on in the life of the project it was decided by the team that the ALAC project was not concerned with the construction of teaching resources that would encourage passive learning (or teaching). We did not want to develop a set of videos, course outlines or teaching schemes that would merely sit on a shelf for occasional use. The aim of the team was to deliver a product that would encourage an active engagement with citizenship on the part of both learner and teacher. Moreover, it was an approach that saw learning as occurring outside the classroom as well as inside and was premised on an enquiry-based learning approach. The development of the project has been an exploration of the process of citizenship education as well as the production of resources that can be used flexibly in different situations.

Active learning is a term that encompasses a wide range of pedagogic approaches which have been used in both schools and universities over a long period. There is evidence that where we wish to engage students so as to encourage their active engagement in a life-long learning process that promotes reflection and the use of higher-order academic skills such as analysis, synthesis and evaluation, this is the path to follow.

Active learning require teachers to reconsider their role and acknowledge that we are all learners involved in a common enterprise and especially so in the area of citizenship. As the National Framework for Active Learning for Active Citizenship (CLG 2006: 10) says,

> This framework does not propose a deficit model, which suggests that only some isolated and inadequate individuals and communities need to learn how to become active citizens. Professionals and policy makers also need to be actively learning about active citizenship, helping society to develop strategies to promote social solidarity and social justice, and learning how to listen to those whose voices are less easily heard. Active learning for active citizenship is for all of us.

Active Citizenship

Active citizenship has become one of the key phrases used in political circles during the past decade. The rights we used to think we had, especially to full employment and a well-funded welfare state, were gradually dismantled during the 1980s by conservative governments in Britain and elsewhere. By the mid-1990s, the centre-left in Britain had ceased talking about the return to significant levels of state intervention and began to talk instead about the benefits of active citizenship. Rather than rely upon the government to see to our every need, we were asked to take responsibility for ourselves and to dedicate at least some of our time and concerns to the broader welfare of the community (see Taylor 2001). Whereas the Conservative governments of the 1980s and early 1990s preached the doctrine of individual self-interest, what became known as New Labour saw in the notion of active citizenship a way to remind us that we are members of communities and that this confers upon us both rights and responsibilities.

Citizenship

Debates on the nature and responsibilities of citizenship have been taking place in political discourse since the time of the Ancient Greeks. The Athenians pioneered a system of direct democracy in which all citizens were invited to participate in public affairs. Whereas Plato dismissed this as the rule of amateurs (Plato 1955), Aristotle recognised that the success and fate of democracy depended upon the quality of its citizens. For Aristotle, citizens have an obligation to cultivate their powers of reason and to participate in the life of the community. Aristotle believed that in doing so citizens can develop and exercise their civic virtues (Aristotle 1912). The Aristotelian view of the relationship between the individual and the community still has relevance today. Although the franchise has been extended far beyond Aristotle's small band of citizens, his belief that human association is natural and that citizens should participate in public affairs can be applied to contemporary society. The Aristotelian tradition sees that through participating in society we develop as citizens and can make significant contributions towards the common good. This line of argument recognises that we need to find ways to reconcile the interests of the individual with those of the collective. It is clear that individuals can and do have a range of private interests that might be inconsistent with those of other members of society. It could be argued, however, that individuals are prone to make serious errors in judgement when they consider their own interests in isolation of any collective interest. If our characters are influenced (or even determined) by our relations with others, then our long-term development rests in no small measure upon the fate of the community.

But how can citizens be encouraged to participate? It could be argued that in a representative democratic system we have representatives to legislate on our behalf and that we are under no obligation to participate politically. It is clear that many people have become alienated from politics and from the political process and that they often feel powerless to the extent that there is 'a chasm opening between government and citizens'

(Civil Renewal Unit 2005: 4). Frazer describes this as a process of 'political disengagement' and argues that if people 'emphasise and underscore their difference from those who typically have political power, that can reinforce any disinclination to participate politically' (2000: 208). Moves to encourage active citizenship can be seen in this political context. The more people disengage, the harder it is for the government to gain compliance and cooperation for its policy agenda. It might therefore be in the interests of governments to get citizens involved in their economic and social programmes. One way of doing this is by using the education system to advance understanding of the responsibilities of citizenship.

Citizenship and Education

Education has numerous social functions. In addition to providing the tools and opportunities for individuals to develop and pursue their interests, educators are often in a position to select and promote a range of social values. When the State has control over the curriculum, these values can be very narrow indeed. One of the great advantages of the higher-education system is that we are at present relatively autonomous. Although there are certainly ways in which our activities are monitored and funnelled through the audit trail, individual academics are still able to investigate diverse value systems and to introduce their students to a broad range of ideas. One of the ways in which we can make a contribution towards the social and political education of our students is to ask them to consider what it is to be a citizen. What are our rights and responsibilities? How can we scrutinise the information we receive and how can we engage in meaningful social reform? These are at least some of the questions that we can ask and address in citizenship education.

In discussing the value of citizenship education, the views of T. H. Marshall and Bernard Crick are particularly important. Although they were primarily interested in using education to promote the virtues of citizenship in the current social and political order, they displayed an interesting degree of respect and sensitivity for their subject matter. Both seemed aware in the language they used and in the warnings they gave that education is a powerful weapon and one that is potentially dangerous. Marshall (1992: 16) argued that education was important for citizenship and that the State should provide education with 'the requirements and the nature of citizenship definitely in mind'. Marshall believed that one of the principal aims of education should be to cultivate the development of citizens and he regarded the right to education as a 'genuine social right of citizenship' (1992: 16). For Bernard Crick, and for his working party on teaching citizenship, citizenship education should help people prepare for adult life. It was not seen as an end in itself but as a means by which we can learn a variety of skills, values and knowledge. It was argued that debate was essential and that we should be willing and able to discuss controversial issues. These debating skills were considered 'vital for a healthy democracy' (Crick 1998: 8). Crick pointed out that the aim of citizenship education should not be to disseminate any set body of knowledge but to develop awareness and understanding of the changing relationship between individuals and government and the changing nature of 'civic cohesion'. In Crick's view, citizenship education should aim to prepare people for 'informed participation' (1998: 14). In this we see an important caveat. Citizenship education should not be about promoting specific values. If it has an over-riding or primary aim it should be to equip people with analytical skills and to encourage us to see ourselves within the context of the community. We need to be able to understand our socio-political environment and to be willing and able to intervene in the political process if moved to do so. Clearly this does not mean that we need to take an active interest in parliamentary politics and in the activities of mainstream political parties. Indeed, to be an active citizen might mean turning our back on such things and associating with smaller groups of people and causes to which we feel some affinity.

Citizenship education in schools is thought to have a number of clear benefits for pupils, schools and for society. In the early stages of discussing the possible shape of citizenship education in Britain, Crick and his team argued that pupils will benefit as citizenship education will help them to become 'active, informed, critical and responsible citizens' (1998: 9). Citizenship education could help schools by forging links between the school and the local community. It was also believed that society will benefit from having 'an active and politically literate citizenry convinced that they can influence government and community affairs at all levels' (Crick 1998: 9). This could, for example, help to make local government 'more democratic, open and responsive' (Crick 1998: 9). Crick recognised that citizenship is given true meaning when it is active. Citizenship is not a single thing. If citizenship is more than the possession of defined rights or a legal status, it is something that is defined and redefined constantly as a result of our own activities.

The Three Themes

The fluid nature of citizenship in general and active citizenship in particular creates a significant challenge for educators. There are many ways in which we can be active, and Crick's recommendations for citizenship education provide us with an interesting place to join the debate. Crick (1998) states that in order to achieve 'effective education for citizenship', it was necessary to explore three main themes:

1. social and moral responsibility;
2. community involvement;
3. political literacy.

It was acknowledged that these themes were 'related to each other' and that they were 'mutually dependent on each other' (Crick 1998: 11). But we can go further than this. Each of Crick's three themes is a form of activity.

Social and moral responsibility calls upon us to think through the implications of our activities upon others. Theorists and practitioners who recognise the importance of the community as a context for individual and social development also see that as individuals we have responsibilities as well as rights. It is thought that these responsibilities should influence the way we interact with fellow members of the community and have an impact upon the demands we place upon the statutory sector. Crick (1998) was clear that he wanted pupils to learn 'socially and morally responsible behaviour' towards each other and towards those in authority. This was proposed in the belief that 'guidance on moral values and personal development are essential preconditions of citizenship' (Crick 1998: 11). It was argued that it is important to encourage a sense of responsibility and that this involved us gaining an understanding of the importance of caring for others, how our actions affect others and that our actions have consequences (Crick 1998: 13). It is believed that by encouraging a sense of social and moral responsibility it might be possible to nurture respect for the rights of others and strengthen the connection between individuals and the communities in which they live.

Crick's second theme, community involvement, invites us to participate in communal endeavours. Marshall recognised that local loyalties are often more important than loyalties towards the national community. Although we might have an obligation to serve the general welfare of the community, this obligation could be a little unrealistic especially if 'the community is so large that the obligation appears remote and unreal' (Marshall 1992: 45). It is possible, however, for schools, colleges and universities to engage with the local community and in so doing help to forge links on a number of levels. Crick (1998) argued that a lot could be learned through working in voluntary groups in the community. In particular, such work could provide people with an insight into the organisation and delivery of public services, the importance of social networks and how to raise funds for community projects (Crick 1998: 12). There are clearly many ways through which universities can also be involved in the community. Work-based learning is becoming increasingly popular. Universities could also draw upon expertise within the local communities and embed this in the courses they offer. Access to higher education could be given to a broad range of students through widening participation programmes. What is important for the development of active citizenship is that universities and their students find ways to engage with the community. In this way, students will gain invaluable skills and experience that could contribute towards community development.

The final theme, political literacy, is likewise active in that it requires us to develop our understanding of the political system and sharpen the tools necessary to make sense of connections within the political process rather than passively assimilate political information. For Crick (1998), becoming politically literate involved such things as gaining a true understanding of how decisions are made, how resources are allocated and how conflicts can be resolved. Indeed, he argued that that political literacy should help pupils 'make themselves effective in public life through knowledge, skills and values' (Crick 1998: 13). It should be noted, however, that political literacy can mean far more than learning how to participate in mainstream politics. It is also possible to gain a great deal from our own political activities, whether this involves participating in the mainstream political process or exerting pressure from the fringes. As active citizens, we need to be able to scrutinise the information we are given, to make sense of the forces at work and, if necessary, to take action. Political literacy is indeed necessary for individuals to engage effectively in the political process. Although the government of the day will not necessarily approve of all forms of political activity, the higher-education system would be in a sorry state indeed if it deferred to any particular government agenda on the nature and scope of true citizenship.

It could be argued that social and political elites have an active interest in keeping citizens passive. We are told in the run-up to general elections that we have the power make a difference, though it is clear that many of the mainstream political parties want to limit this power to selecting who will govern rather having any direct say in determining the priorities of the government. Passive citizens know their place. They tend to their own interests and leave politics to those who are skilled (or foolish) enough to seek public office. Passive citizens may well regard society and political process as external to them and feel that politics is something that is done to them. The current political climate, however, has forced the government to invite citizens to participate in political affairs. It is recognised increasingly that social problems can be alleviated to some extent by involving citizens in the planning and implementation of policies, especially in the areas of community development and crime prevention. The development of active citizenship has the potential to alter the political tone of the age. By empowering citizens to participate in politics, it might even transform for the better the relationship between political parties and the electorate. In the belief that the education system can contribute something towards this, the authors contained within have come together to consider the importance and relationship between active learning and active citizenship.

Conclusion

This monograph is divided into two sections. The first section deals primarily with active learning whilst the main focus of the second section is with active citizenship. This division is made not because we believe that these two things are separate but because we want to adopt different approaches to explore the connections between active learning and active citizenship. By separating the two from the outset, we hope to create a dialectic or battle between active learning and active citizenship in the belief that this will help to generate new ideas and allow the individual authors to see the debate from a distinct point of view. We recognise, moreover, that we cannot leave the two branches of the enquiry in their own distinct pockets and that there must come a point where we look for what unites these ideas. Although a number of the chapters allude to the ways in which active learning and active citizenship are connected, it is in the joint-authored concluding chapter that these connections are explored in depth. In many ways, we do not expect to agree on the nature and potential of active learning and active citizenship. We suggest that it is far more important that we engage in the debate and contribute what we can to the literature than to blunt our differences in the search for consensus.

References

Aristotle (1912) *Politics,* London: Dent.

Arthur, J., Davies, I., Kerr, D. and Wrenn, A. (2001) *Citizenship through Secondary History,* London: RoutledgeFalmer.

Barrows, H. (2007) 'The Minimal Essentials for Problem-based Learning', available at http://www.pbli.org/pbl/pbl_essentials.htm. (Accessed 25 November 2008.)

Biggs, J., (1994) 'Student Learning Research and Theory: Where Do We Currently Stand?' *deliberations.* Available at: http://www.londonmet.ac.uk/deliberations/ocsld-publications/isltp-biggs.cfm. (Accessed 24 February 2009.)

Bussemaker, J (1999) 'Citizenship and Changes in Life-Courses in Post-Industrial Welfare States', in J. Bussemaker (ed.), *Citizenship and Welfare State Reform in Europe,* London: Routledge, pp. 70–84.

California State University Stanislaus (2009) available online at http://www.csustan.edu/ServiceLearning/. (Accessed 25 November 2008.)

Canadian Association For Cooperative Education (CAFCE) (2005) *CAFCE Cooperative Education Manual,* 2nd edn. Available online at http://www.cafce.ca/pages/manual.php. (Accessed 24 November 2008.)

Civil Renewal Unit (2005) *Together We Can,* London: Civil Renewal Unit.

Communities and Local Government (2006) *Take Part: the National Framework for Active Learning for Active Citizenship,* London: Communities and Local Government. Available online at http://www.takepart.org/framework-for-active-learning. (Accessed 20 November 2008.)

Crick, B. (1998) *Education for Citizenship and the Teaching of Democracy in Schools: Final Report of the Advisory Group on Citizenship,* London: Qualifications and Curriculum Authority.

Cronin, A. (2000) *Advertising and Consumer Citizenship,* New York: Routledge.

Crucible Project, available online at http://www.roehampton.ac.uk/crucible/index.html. (Accessed 13 December 2008.)

National Committee of Inquiry into Higher Education (The Dearing Report) (1997) *Higher Education in the Learning Society: The Report of the National Committee of Inquiry into Higher Education,* available online at: https://bei.leeds.ac.uk/Partners/NCIHE/ (Accessed 24 November 2008.)

Felder R. M. and Brent, R. (1994) 'Cooperative Learning in Technical Courses: Procedures, Pitfalls, and Payoffs', available at http://www4.ncsu.edu/unity/lockers/users/f/felder/public/Papers/Coopreport.html.

Felder R. M. and Brent, R. (2003) 'Learning by Doing: The Philosophy and Strategies of Active Learning', *Chemical Engineering Education,* 37 (4): 282–3.

Fink, L. D. (1999) 'Active Learning', available at http://honolulu.hawaii.edu/intranet/committees/FacDevCom/guidebk/teachtip/active.htm (Accessed 20 May 2007.)

Foweraker, J. and Landman, T. (1997) *Citizenship Rights and Social Movements,* Oxford: Oxford University Press.

Frazer, E. (2000) 'Citizenship and Culture', in P. Dunleavy, A. Gamble, R. Heffernan and Peele, G. (eds), *Developments in British Politics 6,* Basingstoke: Macmillan, pp. 203–18.

Huber, M. and Hutching P. (2004) *Integrative Learning: Mapping the Terrain,* Washington, DC: American Association for Colleges and Universities.

Johnson, D., Johnson, R. T. and Stanne, M. B. (2000) 'Cooperative Learning Methods: A Meta-Analysis', available at http://www.co-ooperation.org/pages/cl-methods.html. (Accessed 15 May 2007.)

Justice, C., Warry, W., Cuneo, C., Inglis, S., Miller, S., Rice, J. and Sammon, S. (2001) *A Grammar for Inquiry: Linking Goals and Methods in a Collaboratively Taught Social Sciences Inquiry Course. The Alan Blizzard Award Paper,* Toronto: Society for Teaching and Learning in Higher Education.

Kiviniemi, M. (1999) 'Profiles of Citizenship: Elaboration of a Framework for Empirical Analysis', in J. Bussemaker (ed.), *Citizenship and Welfare State Reform in Europe,* London: Routledge, pp. 114–30.

Little, B. and Harvey, L. (2006) *Learning through Work Placements and Beyond: A Report for HECSU and the Higher Education Academy's Work Placements Organisation Forum,* Sheffield: Centre for Research and Evaluation, Sheffield Hallam University and Centre for Higher Education Research and Information, Open University.

Marshall, T. H. (1992) 'Citizenship and Social Class', in T. H. Marshall and T. Bottomore (eds), *Citizenship and Social Class,* London: Pluto, pp. 3–51. First published 1950.

National Council for Vocational Qualifications (NCVQ) (2005) *Civil Society and Participation: Civil Renewal and Active Citizenship,* London: NCVQ.

Panitz, T. (1996) A Definition of Collaborative vs Cooperative Learning available at http://www.londonmet.ac.uk/deliberations/collaborative-learning/panitz-paper.cfm. (Accessed 15 May 2007.)

Peters, R. S. (1973) 'Farewell to Aims?' *London Educational Review,* 2 (3): 1–4.

Plato (1955) *The Republic,* Harmondsworth: Penguin.

Prince, M. (2004) 'Does Active Learning Work? A Review of the Research', available at http://honolulu.hawaii.edu/intranet/committees/FacDevCom/guidebk/teachtip/active.htm. (Accessed 16 May 2007.)

Schon, D. A. (1987) *Educating the Reflective Practitioner: Towards a New Design for Teaching and Learning in the Professions,* San Francisco, Calif.: Jossey Bass.

Siim, B. (1999) 'Towards a Gender-Sensitive Framework for Citizenship', in J. Bussemaker (ed.), *Citizenship and Welfare State Reform in Europe,* London: Routledge, pp. 85–100.

Taylor, G. (2001) 'The Transformation of Labour', *Contemporary Review,* 278 (February): 65–74.

—— (2007) *Ideology and Welfare,* Basingstoke: Palgrave Macmillan.

Taylor G., Todd, M., McManus, M., Long, J., McCarter R. and Digman, A. (2006) *The Impact of Work Based Learning on Students' Understanding of Citizenship and their Role in the Community,* Southampton: SWAP.

Thirteen ed online (2004) Workshop: Cooperative and Collaborative Learning available at http://www.thirteen.org/edonline/concept2class/index.html. (Accessed 15 May 2007.)

Chapter 2

Active Learning and Active Participation in Higher Education

Yee-Wah Foo, Gary Taylor, Jo Long, Gary Saunders

This chapter examines the reflections, experiences and expectations of students from two British universities who took part in a pilot project to discover what could be gained from getting involved with the design and making of their own seminar programmes. Rather than confine students to the role of consumers of seminar materials, the project was devised to encourage students to be both producers and reflective practitioners. In addition to producing a range of useful resources that could be used on an introductory module on social and political issues, we were interested in exploring the differences between the reflections of the 'producers' and 'consumers' of these seminar materials. Whether they were primarily producers or consumers in this project, the students were asked to reflect upon the value of the resources which were produced and their respective roles in the project. In doing so, they provided some interesting insights into the expectations of students and into the way they view their place in teaching and learning.

Context

The theoretical perspective of active learning in higher education is heavily debated (Rogers 1983; Ramsey and Couch 1994; Hueser 1995; Lonka and Ahola 1995; Burnard 1999; Sander and Stevenson 2000; Taylor 2000; Boud et al. 2001; Brown and Murti 2003; O'Neill and McMahon 2005;

Wingfield and Black 2005), with much of the discussion focusing on the possible benefits of active learning. These include the development of better study skills (Lonka and Ahola 1995), reciprocal peer learning to encourage more effective learning (Boud et al 2001), providing students with a deeper understanding and ability to deal with circumstances in their lives (Hueser 1995), the acquisition of skills that would be useful in the students' future professional careers (Wingfield and Black 2005) and an increase in student participation, motivation and grades (Hall and Saunders 1997).

Rogers (1983: 25, cited in O'Neill and McMahon 2005) describes the theoretical perspective of active learning as being a shift from the focus on an expert teacher dispensing information to greater emphasis being placed on the participation of the student learner, which is driven by the need for a change in the traditional teaching environment where students have become passive, apathetic and bored. This has resulted in a growing number of students feeling they are not being taught or assessed in a way which they would hope to be in higher-education institutions (Sander and Stevenson 2000).

The concept of active learning in higher education has become associated with a plethora of terms, such as self-centred learning, flexible learning (Taylor 2000, cited in O'Neill et al. 2005) and experiential learning (Burnard 1999). However, the definition of all these terms involves students to differing extents, having a greater involvement or participation in their own learning process, rather than merely receiving or observing it (Ramsey and Couch 1994, cited in Brown and Murti 2003: 85). Learning designs that involve active learning provide a more engaged role for learners in the learning process – more so than a passive instructor-centred module design (Wingfield and Black 2005) such as formal lectures, which appear to be almost universally disliked by students and have become increasingly criticised (O'Neill et al. 2005), yet almost universally expected by students in higher education (Sander and Stevenson 2000). Gibbs (1995: 1, cited in O'Neill et al. 2005) describes active participation by students as those courses which allow students to decide 'what is to be learnt, how and when it is to be learnt, with what outcome, what criteria and standards are to be used, how judgements are made and by whom these judgements are made.'

This is not to say that there is a clear delineation between an active learning method and a passive method of teaching. It is perhaps wiser to consider both methods as terms at either end of a continuum, with the possibility of moving further or closer to each method (O'Neill and McMahon 2005). This allows movement from those initiatives that give students complete control over the design of their course and those which offer students no role in module or seminar design.

The benefit of adopting an active learning method is that it is assumed students will learn more effectively and that the learning experience is more intense and permanent (Labinowicz 1980, cited in Wingfield and Black 2005: 119). Not everyone would agree with this premise. It has been argued that deeper levels of involvement by students in course design can result in time being wasted in negotiating the course format, content and requirements and be viewed negatively by both students and academics (Hueser 1995: 588; Mattern 1997: 18). Some students may not have the time (due to other modules on the course or job constraints) to take on the responsibility of designing their own learning (Mattern 1997: 17). It may also be the case that students who have experienced more passive learning designs will reject a more active student approach to learning, be frightened of it (O'Neill et al. 2005) or fail to see why they should take on the responsibility of designing their own learning – a point to be highlighted at a time when students in higher education pay significant tuition fees. Disadvantages have been noted even with a low level of student involvement. For example, contributing in traditional seminars can be perceived as 'brown-nosing', unnecessarily extending seminars and resulting in small group activities turning into social sessions (Brown and Murti 2003: 85). It could be that active learning is more effective with postgraduates than undergraduates (Brown and Murti 2003: 88), possibly due to a more mature approach to study. Mattern (1997) suggests that active learning may be more appropriate and indeed more effective for certain academic courses than others. For example, he points out that democratising the learning process whilst teaching democratic theory, can give students practical experience of democracy for reflection and analysis.

Research has shown that although there are pitfalls when involving students in designing and running modules, students and staff can still gain a great deal from participating in course design. A number of studies suggest that the active participation of students in the design process can have a beneficial impact upon self-directed learning (Cheng and Coombs 2001), have enduring effects and implications for lifelong learning (Brown and Murti 2003: 86) and enhance the relationships between students and tutors (Hudson et al. 2003). As Brown and Murti (2003: 85–6) noticed, it is possible for students to become involved in planning and designing seminars or even the whole course, thus becoming partners instead of subordinates in the learning process. Furthermore, most modules can be structured so that they offer students at least some active participation in the learning process.

There are, of course, many ways to characterise active participation. The notion of participative learning (see Wingfield and Black 2005) is particularly useful in recognising the importance of allowing students some degree of control in designing modules and courses. The extent and character of this control can vary greatly and include ambitious programmes (often at postgraduate level) where students design their own learning outcomes and course structure. It can also embrace more modest ventures (often at undergraduate level) where students are asked to take part in determining the direction and focus of a pre-existing module. Both types of endeavour, stimulating in their own ways, can be seen to provide a context for the present study.

Examples of the more ambitious approach can be seen in a postgraduate programme offered at Glasgow Caledonian University where, on a work-based degree, students defined their own goals and designed their own programme of study. These students were allowed to submit case studies from their work as the major components of their degree. Although mentors at work supervised them, academics remained involved to ensure the maintenance of academic quality and standards (Sander and Stevenson 2000: 1). Other innovative projects include involving students in formulating a postgraduate programme on educational design. In this project, students were required to establish the syllabus that members of staff would teach the following year (see Koelher et al. 2004). These projects have in common a willingness to transfer the power of establishing the framework and rationale for a course to the students. Although students would no doubt continue to consume academic resources, they were not regarded in the slightest as passive consumers of knowledge. Their participation extended far beyond choosing between a few alternatives at the fringes of the course. Indeed, these projects allowed students to have a real say in what they were taught and to express their own needs in a fundamental and largely uncensored way.

Participative ventures developed at undergraduate level often involve students helping to design aspects of a module and working within a broad framework set by members of staff. An example of this can be seen in the work of Heuser (1995) who involved students in the design and teaching of a module on death studies. The tutor established a broad framework for the module but the students were allowed to choose the specific content to be covered. The students identified six main areas that they wanted to cover. The tutor agreed to deliver material on two of the areas, leaving the remaining four to be researched and delivered by students working in small groups. Heuser found that students were extremely creative in the methods they used to present the material. These methods included the use of their own drawings, reading poetry and singing songs. Left to their own devices, students will often put a lot of thought into the way they present lecture or seminar materials. Rarely do they seek to copy their tutor. Because of this, tutors can often learn a great deal from student presentations on the preferences and expectations of their students.

Although some of the literature shows that students do not necessarily gain higher (or indeed lower) marks when they engage in experimental or participative learning programmes (see Wingfield and Black 2005), there are many other ways for students to benefit from their involvement in such schemes. As we have seen, Brown and Murti (2003) found that involving students increased levels of attendance and the motivation of their students. Heuser believed that students can prosper in a supportive and collaborative environment and that this can often lead to a 'rich exchange of ideas' (1995: 588). It was noted by Koehler et al. (2004) that students who participate in course design enter into different relationships with their tutors and often gain considerably in confidence. Staff can likewise feel the benefits. It has been argued that the active participation of students in course design can also be beneficial in democratising education (Heuser 1995; Mattern 1997) and in the development of new pedagogy (Hudson et al. 2002). It is also apparent that staff can use such schemes to gain an insight into the needs and expectations of their students. Indeed, it has been argued that those involved in education should be willing to ascertain the expectations of their students and 'find the best learning route for each cohort of students' (Sander and Stevenson 2000: 1). It would appear that the literature supports the view that involving students in the design and teaching of modules can be rewarding for all concerned. Following on from this, our project seeks to investigate what can be gained by involving students in the production of seminar materials.

Method

The aim of our project was to get staff and students at two universities involved in designing and applying seminar materials for a first year module on the 'Politics of Everyday Life'. The lectures were set by staff at University B, and the seminar questions set by staff at University A. Seminar materials were produced by students at University A and used by students at University B (see below).

University A Staff	Prepared seminar questions
University B Staff	Prepared lectures
University A Students	Prepared seminar materials
University B Students	Used seminar materials

The module ran for one semester, and the seminar programme was designed to cover five main areas:

1. democracy;
2. the media;
3. religious fundamentalism;
4. pressure groups;
5. the environment.

Two weeks was dedicated to each area. In each case, the students received lectures and were required to prepare for the seminars using materials prepared by students at another university.

Seminar materials were created by a student citizenship forum established at University A and consisting of seven students, four from Year 2 and three from Year 3. Year 2 students were invited to participate because they had recent experience of studying at Year 1. It was hoped that involving Year 3 students would benefit the project because of their greater experience of studying in higher education. These students were paid a small fee for participating in the project and were asked to produce seminar materials on the issues outlined above. The students were divided into three groups (with at least two students in each group), and each group was given a distinct question to address on each of the topics. Members of the forum were asked to produce different types of resources including lists of weblinks with brief commentaries, reviews of websites, raw material derived from questionnaires and transcripts of short interviews. The types of materials differed according to the topic under discussion, and various research techniques were used to challenge both the producers and the consumers of the seminar programme.

By way of illustration, what follows is a brief description of the resources produced for the session on democracy. Members of the forum were asked to produce a list of weblinks with short descriptions of each site. A total of sixty-three sites were selected in response to three questions:

1. **To what extent can democracy be defined?** Students in Group 1 selected thirty sites. These sites included those of campaigning groups (e.g., Charter 88, Transparency International), media outlets and those covering international perspectives (e.g., USA, Canada, Latin America) and critical perspectives (e.g., Islamic).

2. **To what extent does democracy threaten the interests of the minority?** Students in Group 2 selected thirteen sites which included speeches, books and extracts from such authors as Samuel Brittan and the sites of marginalised groups who claim that their interests are being ignored (e.g., supporters of fox hunting).

3. **To what extent are elites necessary to run the political system?** Students in Group 3 selected twenty sites that covered media critiques of politicians for being out of touch with the views of the electorate, intellectual critiques of elite agendas (e.g., the works of Frank Furedi) and a collection of right- and left-wing critiques of the political centre.

The material varied greatly in terms of analytical depth, topicality and political colour. The consumers of these resources would therefore have a great deal of choice in the types of material they could use.

The materials produced by the Student Citizenship Forum were used by two seminar groups at University B. Each group was divided into three sections, with at least four students in each section. Having prepared notes with the materials before the seminar session, the groups were asked to discuss their findings during the seminar and to record their conclusions on flip charts. The findings of each group were then shared with the rest of the class in the form of mini-presentations.

The project was not only concerned with the production and consumption of seminar materials but also with encouraging the students to reflect upon the value of the material. Members of the Student Citizenship Forum (at University A) were asked to reflect upon what they learned not only about the topics but also about constructing a seminar programme. The students at University B were asked to reflect upon the choices they made in their use of the forum material. In this way, we hoped to gain an insight into what the students valued. It is this reflective element that is the primary focus of the current paper.

The Producers

Rather than outline in any detail what the Student Citizenship Forum produced, we are primarily interested in uncovering what the students learned about the art of constructing seminar programmes. Many members of the forum recognised that it was important to identify a range of sources in the hope of appealing to a variety of users. Forum Member A tried to provide 'a wide and sometimes provocative range of opinions and viewpoints'. One of the group recognised that it was important to be open-minded when devising a programme for other students, though she also noted that she found it difficult to understand how some of these views are sustained in modern society (Forum Member F). Another member argued that it was important to provide students with a variety of views and to try to provide balance in the selection of websites. In his view, the web is dominated by radical groups but that it was surprisingly difficult to find material on the far right of the political spectrum and that the sites that existed 'tended to be in disrepair and quite small' (Forum Member G). He went on to argue that left-wing sites were considerably more numerous and better maintained. He felt that this might be because the political left (in Britain at least) is 'more intellectually appealing' than the political right (Forum Member G).

Members of the Student Citizenship Forum identified a number of problems that they encountered whilst searching for material to use in the seminar programme. It was noted that there was some difficulty finding good quality material and arranging this in a logical fashion (Forum Member A). One member of the group complained about having to wade through 'useless information' (Forum Member B). It was also noted that it was difficult to find neutral websites, with the exception of sites like wikipedia (Forum Member A). Another member of the forum felt that it was difficult to provide neutral descriptions of the resources he found, and he recognised that this was in part because the issues covered tended to be quite emotive. He asked, for example, whether the BNP (British National Party) should be described as a 'nationalist' or a 'racist' party. He felt that there were problems with describing the BNP as a racist party because it would 'not provide students with an opportunity to formulate their own opinions' (Forum Member G). It would seem, indeed, that students were aware that they had a responsibility to test the quality of the materials they selected and that political neutrality was something to be aspired to in the presentation of this material. They were clearly interested in providing room for diverse opinions whilst not wanting to be open about where they stood on an issue by skewing the selection of material in favour of any particular faction or political ideology.

The students were quite open about their desires to produce something that would benefit other students. One member of the forum hoped that by engaging in a 'critique', other students could in turn develop their own understanding of the topics (Forum Member C). It was argued that the project was useful because 'it gives an insight from other students, perhaps giving a slant as to ways of examining topics' (Forum Member E). Forum Member D recalled how she struggled with some parts of the project and she was 'worried that parts of my work will be useless'. At the same time, however, she felt that the topics covered were important because they had an impact upon us all and that, because of this, 'the information presented should in theory interest everybody' (Forum Member D). Members of the forum seemed to believe that they had plenty to offer to other students and that the seminar programme they helped to construct would, by definition, be student-friendly.

Members of the forum claimed that they learned a great deal from participating in the project. Some of the group viewed what they learned very much in terms of their own skills development. Forum Member B identified greater confidence in approaching students to gain their cooperation and improvements in her own communication skills as the main things she had learned. Forum Member C talked about improvements in his time management and the benefits he derived from using different research methods. Forum Member F noted that the project drew upon and helped to develop her analytical skills. Another member of the forum valued the project because it allowed him to learn about new topics and gauge his understanding of more familiar topics. He believed that it had provided him with 'a chance to think about what I would like to know about the subject and what would challenge me if I were to study the area further' (Forum Member G). The diverse range of topics was particularly appealing, partly because the members of the forum knew that they could concentrate upon the topics they found most interesting and ignore those that they had little interest in.

The students engaged in producing seminar materials also learned a lot about the art of producing seminar programmes. Forum Member D seemed to learn some interesting lessons about empathy. She said that she learned 'how to view the resources I found from differing perspectives' (Forum Member D) and that the project 'required me to think about what other students might think about the topic under investigation' (Forum Member D). It was noted that in devising a seminar programme it was important to 'be consciously aware that you are not the target audience and that the readers (in this case other students) are the main priority' (Forum Member F). These students recognised that they were the 'tutors' and that they needed to give at least some thought to the possible interests and reactions of their 'students'. Through producing resources for other students, they managed to get a glimpse of how many tutors attempt to gauge the interests and dispositions of their students and, in so doing, that they had responsibilities towards their students. In particular, they saw that they needed to incorporate different perspectives on the topics under discussion so as to increase the chances of engaging their students.

In addition to recognising the importance of producing diverse materials, members of the forum wanted to avoid providing their students with all that they need and to find ways to stimulate their students' learning. Forum Member A said that 'I have learnt to think in terms of providing "starting points" for discussion, rather than a fixed curriculum learning programme'. He claimed that we should always avoid providing students with information to 'bank' in a passive way and that he 'worked upon the assumption that they would take on an active learning approach, following up leads and ideas' (Forum Member A). This view was also echoed in the reflections of Forum Member E. She believed that it was not necessary to provide the students with all the facts or all of the perspectives and that it was more important to provide 'an entry point to the more complicated aspects, developing the student's thought and rationalising process'. Forum Member F hoped that what she had provided might 'open some people's minds to new phenomena' and that the resources she helped to create should be used by students as a foundation to 'actively seek out further knowledge to broaden their understanding'. This member of the group tried to avoid settling for bland material and was convinced that we should avoid spoon-feeding the students and should aspire to 'interest the reader enough to investigate further and provide them with enough knowledge to discuss the issues and generate further questions and arguments' (Forum Member F). It is apparent that for these students it is more important to stimulate students into exploring their interests than to provide answers to all of the questions raised in a topic or module.

It could be argued that the project provided too much for students. Indeed, some members of the forum seemed to have reservations about the amount of detail they were asked to provide. Forum Member A warned that a rigid and prescriptive approach could place unnecessary limits on discussion and 'stifle the sort of exploration of issues and making of connections, which is absolutely necessary in the social sciences' (Forum Member A). In addition to clarifying his own understanding of the issues, he claimed that the project had helped to convince him that the 'best way to learn is to be involved in teaching' (Forum Member A). Forum Member G noted that although the project had 'stretched' his research skills, he felt that it would be 'a shame to provide first-year students with a list of sites already identified by somebody else, as they would miss out on the opportunity to develop the skills needed to search for them on their own' (Forum Member G). In his view, providing such materials and guidance could be useful in the short term but 'in the medium to long term I feel it would be detrimental to their learning experience' (Forum Member G). Herein lies an illustration that students can learn a great deal about active learning by taking part in designing seminar programmes. Involving students in the construction of our modules can indeed provide an arena for students to explore their interests in an active way. Perhaps we need to think more in terms of teaching our students to teach rather than to learn.

The Consumers

In addition to gaining some understanding of the motives, hopes and fears of the producers, we recognised that it was also important to allow plenty of room for the consumers to evaluate the materials that had been produced for them. We were aware that the project could backfire if the consumers took exception to using materials produced by other students. We found, however, that there were no objections voiced to using materials produced by other students. If anything, the students seemed genuinely pleased that the Student Citizenship Forum had made the effort to provide them with detailed explanations of many of the sources. Group Member 2B appreciated that 'websites were explained so I knew what they were about'. When asked to evaluate what was liked most about the module, many students commented that the module was constructively designed. 'Seminars and lectures combined to provide an effective learning method' (Evaluation A). 'Lectures and seminars linked well' (Evaluation B). Although one student said he did not enjoy the group work, he still felt that the module was 'pro-active' and that he 'always felt involved' (Evaluation

G). The students seemed to have no objection to using materials produced by other students and felt that these materials were well designed and had even fostered a sense of inclusiveness.

It was clear from the evaluations we conducted that the students at University B appreciated having access to a wide variety of viewpoints. As consumers, they felt it was essential to have 'a wide variety of views' (Group Member 1I) from a 'wide range of sources' (Group Member 1G). Although one group member argued that several of the sources 'appeared biased' (Group Member 2D) and another student warned against the use of extremist sites (Evaluation M), it was conceded that a full range of views was still beneficial. For example, Group Member 2A was of the opinion that even though she 'may not agree with the views expressed', such a broad selection to choose from meant that she could 'create a better argument'. It was apparent to some of the students that a number of sites lacked political neutrality. Remarkably, their reflections show this was not found to be a disadvantage but, rather, an opportunity to learn something new and gain further insight. Group Member 1E chose what he considered to be the most radical sites because he thought 'they would represent the more interesting and controversial points of view'. Many of the students actively picked out different or unusual sites. Group Member 3F wanted to use 'the most controversial sites – politically, religiously and racially'. Rather than looking for political neutrality, the students searched for diversity and were open-minded about radical interpretations, no matter how provocative.

We were also interested to find out how useful students at University B found the materials produced by students in the forum. We found that the students could be extremely critical if certain selections were 'not useful' (Group Member 1C) and they took for granted that the materials should be of a professional standard (Group Members 1F and 1B). The students fully expected to do further research on their own initiatives, and they welcomed thought-provoking information that was 'not normally accessed by the public' (Group Member 1F). The students also seemed to like how the materials suited a diverse range of levels. Some of the lesser-prepared students admitted that it was necessary sometimes to access information quickly to survive a seminar. One of the students claimed that 'I knew Wikipedia would be easy to understand' and give me what 'I needed to know' (Group Member 3G). Other students preferred material with more depth. For example, Group Member 1C specifically chose selections with 'a good range of intellectual opinion'. Group Member 2A picked sites with 'alternative and quirky initiatives'. The materials were gauged at the right level and catered for different needs. Catering for different levels and providing materials that expressed a diverse range of opinions seemed to engage the students in a very real way. Far from being passive receivers, the students at University B were keen to get involved in an active way. Nobody wanted to be 'spoon-fed'. Student Aa, for example, claimed that the project provided 'a very useful method of studying new material because rather than simply listening to a lecture and taking notes, then doing nothing until a seminar on the same subject, active learning required me to find material myself and engage with it' (Assessment A). The level of engagement did of course very between the students, but there were definite signs that involving students in the production of seminar materials had helped to engage the vast majority on one level or another.

We found that the project did have a beneficial impact upon student satisfaction and attainment on the module. The students placed a high value on being able to do well in the seminar presentations, so it was important to them that the research they carried out was relevant to their tasks (Group Members 1E and 2A). They also valued being able to debate during the seminar on a variety of controversial issues (Assessments E and J). The students appreciated doing something 'different'. One of the students pointed out that the module 'was different to all other modules I have studied this semester and offered some variation to the course . . . as well as improving my debating skills' (Assessment J). The assessment – another important factor for the students – was to choose one of the topics covered in the seminars and to consider the contemporary resonance of the topic. Although studies by Wingfield and Black (2005) show that students do not necessarily gain higher or lower marks when they engage in participative learning programmes, the assessment marks for the groups concerned were extremely encouraging. One third of the students attained a first. The average mark was 62 per cent, and there were no fails.

Conclusion

In writing this paper we were particularly interested in comparing the reflections of the producers and consumers of seminar materials. Both groups can teach us about the expectations and experiences of students using electronic sources for seminar preparation. Rather than comment on all of the comments and differences, in this conclusion we are going to concentrate upon what the producers and consumers of the resources had to say about the variety and neutrality of sources and their views on the value of the project.

Both the producers and the consumers placed a high value upon producing or having access to a wide variety of sources. Although it might be tempting as tutors to channel the attention of our students to a few key sources, it is clear that many of the students who took part in our project want the freedom to judge for themselves what is attractive or useful. For the producers, this variety was viewed in terms of allowing room for different points of view and different political persuasions. Although the consumers also wanted different perspectives, they also noted the importance of having access to materials of different levels of complexity. It was clear that for the consumers of seminar materials, it is important that we recognise different levels of interest, ability or time when we construct our seminars. Although we might want all of our students to read theoretically sophisticated material, not all of them will have the time or interest to do so. If we fail to cater for these students, it could be argued that we run the risk of allowing them to remain relatively disengaged from the module. The inclusion of some basic sources, as long as they are acknowledged as such, might help to keep the less motivated on board.

The issue of neutrality was raised by both the producers and the consumers. The web is renowned for attracting marginalised groups and for its radical spirit. It could be argued indeed that an author writing for the web has no real responsibility to produce a balanced product. Because of this, the Internet is seemingly full of extreme views. This was clearly something that worried the producers of the resources. A number of them worried that they were unable to find neutral sites or use neutral terms to describe what they found. The consumers, however, were rather less concerned with this. As long as there was choice, the students felt that they could judge for themselves. It would appear that the students who consumed the materials did not expect neutrality and were content to balance arguments for themselves using a diverse range of opinions.

When asked to consider the value of the project, the differences between the producers and the consumers became apparent. The consumers evidently viewed the project in fairly instrumental terms. In particular, they appreciated the work of the producers because it provided them with accessible advice and because there were plenty of interesting selections that could help them prepare seminar presentations and fuel seminar debates. The producers, however, seemed quite surprised that what they gained was an insight into the activities and to some extent value structure of tutors. When the producers reflected on their experience, they talked about having to empathise with other students and to gauge their interests. In addition, they recognised that they had responsibilities towards their audience. These responsibilities included finding ways to stimulate interest in the subject, encourage others to explore things for themselves rather than expect to be spoon-fed and allowing enough room for students to develop their own views. In so doing, the producers used their experience of consuming resources to develop interesting resources for others to consume. This, we suppose, is where we all start. The trick, however, is to find ways to maintain this commitment.

References

Brown, R. and Murti, G. (2003) 'Student Partners in Instruction: Third Level Student Participation in Advanced Business Courses', *Journal of Education for Business,* 79 (2): 85–9.

Boud, D., Cohen, R. and Sampson, J. (2001) *Peer Learning in Higher Education: Learning from and with Each Other,* London: Routledge.

Burnard, P. (1999) 'Carl Rogers and Postmodernism: Challenges in Nursing and Health Sciences', *Nursing and Health Sciences* 1: 241–7.

Cheng, V. and Coombs, S. (2001) 'The Experience of Self-Organised Learning through the Use of Learning Plans for Knowledge Management', paper presentation at the 8th Annual EDINEB International Conference: Technology, Pedagogy and Innovation, Nice, France, June.

Gibbs, G. (1995) *Assessing Student Centred Courses,* Oxford: Oxford Centre for Staff Learning and Development.

Hall, J. and Saunders, P. (1997) 'Adopting a Student-Centred Approach to Management of Learning', in C. Bell, M. Bowden and A. Trott (eds), *Implementing Flexible Learning,* London: Kogan Page, pp. 85–94.

Heuser, L. (1995) 'Death Education: A Model of Student-Participatory Learning', *Death Studies,* 19 (6): 583–90.

Hudson, B., Hudson, A. and Steel, J. (2002) 'Orchestrating Interdependence in a Multinational Virtual Learning Community', paper presented at European Conference on Educational Research, University of Lisbon, September.

Hudson, B., Owen, D. and Veen, K. van (2003) 'Working on Educational Research Methods with Masters Students in an International Online Learning Community', paper to the EERA Network 6 Open Learning Contexts, Cultural Diversity, Democracy (OPENnet), European Conference on Educational Research, University of Hamburg, September.

Kereki, I. F. de, Azpiazu, J. and Silva, A. (2003) 'A New Learning Environment Model Based on Knowledge Management and Its Use in University Teaching', paper presented at European Conference on Educational Research, University of Hamburg, September.

Koehler, M., Mishra, P., Hershey, K. and Peruski, L. (2004) 'With a Little Help from Your Students: A New Model for Faculty Development and Online Course Design', *Journal of Technology and Teacher Education,* 12 (1): 25–55.

Labinowicz, E. (1980) *The Piaget Primer: Thinking, Learning, Teaching,* Menlo Park, Calif.: Addison-Wesley Publishing Co.

Lizzio, A. and Wilson, K. (2004) 'Action Learning in Higher Education: An Investigation of Its Potential to Develop Professional Capability', *Studies of Higher Education,* 29 (4): 469–88.

Lonka, K. and Ahola, K. (1995) 'Activating Instruction: How to Foster Study and Thinking Skills in Higher Education', *European Journal of Psychology of Education,* 10: 351–68.

Mattern, M. (1997) 'Teaching Democratic Theory Democratically', *Political Science and Politics,* 30 (3): 510–15.

O'Neill, G. and McMahon, T. (2005) 'Student-Centred Learning: What Does It Mean for Students and Lecturers?', *Emerging Issues in the Practice of University Learning and Teaching,* available at http://www.aishe.org/readings2005–1 (accessed 12 March 2007).

Quarstein, V. and Peterson, P. (2001) 'Assessment of Cooperative Learning: A Goal Criterion Approach', *Innovative Higher Education,* 26 (1): 59–77.

Ramsey, V. J. and Couch, P. D. (1994) 'Beyond Self-Directed Learning: a Partnership Model of Teaching and Learning', *Journal of Management Education,* 18: 139–63.

Rogers, C. R. (1983) *Freedom to Learn for the 80s,* Columbus, Ohio: Charles Merrill.

Rovai, A. (2003) 'A Practical Framework for Evaluating Online Distance Education Programs', *Internet and Higher Education,* 6 (2): 109–24.

Sander, P. and Stevenson, K. (2000) 'How to Save Students from Boredom', *Times Higher Education Supplement,* available online at http://www.thes.co.uk/search/story.aspx?story_id=64167 (accessed 10 April 2006).

Taylor, P. G. (2000) 'Changing Expectations: Preparing Students for Flexible Learning', *The International Journal of Academic Development,* 5 (2): 107–15.

Wingfield, S. and Black, G. (2005) 'Active Versus Passive Course Designs: The Impact on Student Outcomes', *Journal of Education for Business,* 81 (2): 119–23.

Chapter 3

The Role of Rich Media in Active Learning and a Learner-Centred Approach

Richard McCarter

There are different ways to create learning experiences and interact with our physical environment (Beard and Wilson 2001), and it is often the teacher's task to create the conditions for this interaction to take place. Rich media in education, whether video, audio or animation, which is either delivered over the web, broadcast or distributed on CD-ROM, has often been used for presenting ambiguous or real world events whereby learners extract information for their own interpretation (Bates 2005). The learning can be more challenging when faced with abstract subject matter in rich media form. According to Dale, cited in Spencer (1988), there are a total of ten human experiences, and interaction with our physical environment contributes to the broadest of these experiences. The term 'motion picture' is placed seventh. However, the use of digital technology offers new opportunities for the learner to interact with each other and the learning environment and any online resources available. So what happens to learning and the learning process when these two experiences are combined – in effect bringing a real-world event and rich media together? Can the viewing or listening behaviour of our learners be altered with rich media? Can we use the rich media for a more active experience? To what extent can the learner make the video material adaptive and with open access and presentational media being available, is the learner encouraged to be more responsive to what they find even if the medium is not responsive to their actions? This chapter explores the potential for rich media in both linear and non-linear form to create the learning conditions to stimulate different forms of learning 'activity', whether through a 'doing' experience, whereby learners experience an actual activity, or through 'active sense-making', whereby learners test out their interpretations, or learning through a set of 'activities' or tasks.

Learning with Rich Media: The Linear Mode

Let's consider the linear narrative aspects of television and video and an understanding of what is meant by 'activity'. Active learning happens when students engage in a more interactive relationship with the subject matter of a course, encouraging them to generate rather than simply to receive knowledge. In an active learning setting can a piece of rich media of a real-world case study deliver an activity? The different forms of activity can be characterised through notions of 'active learning', 'active sense making' and learning through a set of 'activities' or tasks. The rich media could be a piece of learning material (uni-dimensional organisation of a resource) such as video. As the content in the video increases in complexity, the linear mode can become ill structured, and increasing amounts of important information are lost (Spiro and Jehng 1990).

In an evaluation of teachers using a video resource; the subject of which was children doing mathematics (Laurillard 2002) a number of effects on student learning was noted. Firstly, the video had the effect of allowing students to respond to the stimulus of real life, (the problems of doing maths) and secondly, it provided the students with a critical appreciation of these problems. The evaluation arrived at the conclusion that learners wanted time to 'sense' (2002: 104) the media text and also a period of time to develop a critical appreciation. This was defined as a form of 'active' video (2002: 104) whereby the students felt the need to be supported when they wanted a response to the observations and the questions that they had raised after viewing.

In the studies of learning behaviour and linear modes of learning carried out at the British Open University, the use of video was seen as problematic for some learners. Although video was accepted as a useful vehicle for mass education, there was concern that delivery was of an unsuitable pace and that the visually orientated learner might be at a disadvantage.

Bates (1983) has framed the difficulties of using video through his experiences at the Open University. One of these experiences studied the effects of the learner studying in isolation and the outcome of this was to offer a number of warnings; these warnings described the unsuccessful features of Open University television programme because students have shown to have many different learning characteristics and also different media preferences.

In a live broadcast, some students would find the pace difficult. There would be some learners watching, who would be viewing the content but be out of synchronisation with the corresponding text because they found themselves two weeks behind with the readings. The VHS video-cassette player and recorder gave the learner the ability to control the pace, which overcame the scheduling problem, yet still it was considered that visual information was more difficult to code, the target audience varied considerably, learners had problems with pace, and suitability was questioned due to general ability.

The British Open University provided a wide range of media on the basis that each student was likely to find at least one means which he or she felt comfortable with in their learning. In many of their studies on the effects of video, they found that video can be more helpful to 'weak' students than to successful students. Gallagher's research (Bates 1987) identified the characteristics or learning traits of Open University students. These traits placed students in one of three categories. There were learners who wanted the 'straight instruction', which the research team referred to as the 'didacticists'; there were learners who were less confident in their approach and referred to as 'guidance seekers', and there were learners who were happy to be 'explorers' and understood the purpose of the materials being presented to them.

Cenammo (1993) also makes a contribution to the theory on mental processing by suggesting that only certain skills can be learnt from television. The studies show that breakdowns in comprehension occur when additional effort is expended in order to understand complex narration and visuals. The studies show that a high degree of corresponding narration with pictures, where both the narration and the text closely match thematically, often leads to learners exerting more effort. The value of video became increasing apparent in the past fifteen years through the laser-disc multimedia application – partly to teach skills (instructional activity) and partly to train academic thought. Since streamed video became technically possible in the latter part of the 1990s, much of this interaction, control of pace and the introduction of self-assessment questions was used to enhance the learning without making costly changes to the delivery platform and the hundreds of CD-ROMs (for distribution). The benefit to learners was that pace and assessment was built in.

There is an added concern, that once learners had become adept at using an image-rich environment, which offers an alternative to traditional text-based learning (McFarland 1996), they would continue to use images to support learning. Learners often associated video with low levels of mental effort (Salomon 1984), and the obvious solution would be to combine still and moving images with text.

In a study of children between the ages of ten to twelve (Feuerstein 1999), researchers discovered a reversal of this situation. In the research, rich media was being used as a tool for active learning as well as knowledge acquisition. There was intensive teaching of media literacy skills to a group of medium to low achieving pupils. The assessment tests that followed showed that this group improved substantially their media literacy and critical thinking skills. Although it is worth pointing out that the control groups of high achieving pupils, who received far less instruction, did not show such high gains in critical thinking skills, it appears that the intensive training given by teachers on media literacy combined with the active experience of making videos for a school competition substantially increased the pupils' critical thinking skills - far more so than their high achieving counterparts. It was felt that the increased instruction and the experience of making videos allowed them to develop their media language and so improve their negotiation of meaning of media literacy and production of media.

Video conferencing is a linear medium and also synchronous communication. Although the medium is a live event, it does not always allow the learner time for individual cognitive processing – the ability to pause discussion, to analyse a picture, to reflect or to capture the effects of social interaction. An online text-based discussion forum can be asynchronous and synchronous, but as Laurillard (2002) explains, video conferencing can be very teacher-centred; here (as in a lecture theatre), there is less opportunity for social interaction, creating the sense that it is not a very discursive medium despite the fact that it delivers audio and video.

Video and the Digital Age

So, what can be achieved by using video in digital form, on demand and available in multimedia form and not necessarily with an emphasis on the narrative or its linear mode? New forms of non-linear and multi-dimensional learning such as multimedia, present to the learner the options for a random access approach. They are afforded the ability to be supported through a variety of media, with the added bonus of pace and flexibility; being able to revisit materials in a variety of different contexts.

Let us consider the approaches taken by educational multimedia developers and computer-based packages which have embedded rich media in their design structure in order to create a range of learning experiences. Whilst these applications do not entertain notions of participation, ownership of learning, community, collaboration and reflection, they are dealing with features of increased interactivity and learner activity. Interactivity now has new meaning; the term describes the function whereby the user can navigate and select content at will, whether text, audio, graphics, video or any combination of these.

Many computer and multimedia systems are didactic in nature. They are instructional learning resources and are based on models of learning where knowledge transmission such as drill and practice and repetition are the guiding educational factors. Small chunks of information are presented to learners in a predetermined order, and learners work from one 'chunk' to the next. Mayer (2005) adds that multimedia materials and active learning are designed to prime behavioural learning. In his work on the use of multimedia and cognitive processes he makes a careful distinction between behavioural activity and cognitive activity. The latter is described as *meaningful learning* (2005: 14) whereupon a learner interrogates and re-orders content in an attempt to gain a complete a picture and a new mental representation of the materials being presented. This is his definition of active learning.

Laurillard (2002) explores the tension between video as a passive experience and video as an interactive one and looks for models of learning that are using an active learning approach where the objective is to link different media in an interactive multimedia form. In order to help assess the value of these different ways for the learner to engage in an activity and to be active, it is worth referring to Laurillard (1995) and the changing experiences of the learner when using a multimedia presentation. The narrative medium, as typified by using video to take the learner in a general direction of learning – the authorial voice, dictating the route to the goal and deciding on when this goal has been reached, requires the learner to take part as the listener and the teacher places him or herself in the role of storyteller, emphasising that it is a teacher-constructed world that is being created but that the learner, despite having access to this 'narrative line' (1995: 188) is able to construct their own analysis before accessing the expert's analysis. It is common for educators to look for ways to turn existing materials into multimedia form as this is can be a convenient way to exploit digital technology and new media with the already prevalent print and audio-visual materials. Laurillard (1995) warns of the paradox whereby the multimedia product is so complex that less confident learners (less skilled in research and data handling) actually miss out on learning due to their inability to complete a range of tasks; that learners cannot set appropriate goals or are unsure how to evaluate the information that they find. This is referred to as 'discovery learning' whereby the learner is interacting with the teacher-constructed world as though the learner was on a field trip or attempting a classroom experiment, but only extensive teacher input in the form of preparation, supervision and de-briefing can support the learner. If this is not addressed, the learner cannot direct their own learning. In Laurillard's view, there are many educators who believe that discovery learning is over-ambitious and most learners are not ready to be 'researchers' (1995: 186). Since we have already learnt that the narrative structures in linear forms of rich media form can be complex, the learning approach must change so that the learning design features must mirror what the learner must do and how the teacher supports; that there is an opportunity for reflection where the learner needs to consider the implications of their experiences. Therefore the narrative aspects of a multimedia package require a different strategy. The objective of this approach that Laurillard (1995) refers to as 'guided discovery' (1995: 186) has a different kind of structure and approach where the teacher guides, advises and comments on progress. When the teacher isn't present, the learner becomes a researcher by studying a database of rich media objects. In a multimedia form, guided discovery attempts to maintain the clear value of a narrative line whilst allowing the learner a fair degree of learner control, but with a clear objective which does not allow the learner to wander aimlessly through an 'unfathomable' (1995: 189) database of resources. The learner is still allowed to construct their own approach.

It makes sense to review the advice on text-based materials and to combine this with essential matters on the design and implementation of multimedia applications. Lockwood (1992) offers us an insight into how the writers at the British Open University have viewed learning activities. This insight offers further practical guidance on how rich media can enhance the learning experience. First, he draws upon the know-how of those writing materials that cover different intellectual levels as well as subjects. The materials are described in the form of either a linear programme or a branching programme of learning. The basic premise is that when writing for distance learners, the idea is to encourage learners to respond to the text rather than to remain passive.

There are pitfalls to attempting to create 'active learners' using hypermedia or multimedia applications. Lockwood (1992) asks writers to imagine a learner and to describe the ideal form of teaching that would take place. To create an analogy with the classroom situation, Lockwood introduces the 'Reflective Action Guide' (1992: 114) whereby students operate outside the confines of the text, reflect on their actions and look for unique situations.

Clarke's text on writing for computer-based learning (2001) makes a valuable point that there is a danger of overloading the learner by making the environment too rich and exciting that learners are unable to sort through the content and identify the key issues in the mass of information. Race (1996) has identified the disadvantages to some kinds of applications, the main ones being that students using print-based materials do not feel a sense of ownership to the solutions to their own problems. When using interactive print resources, it is too easy for students to skip exercises. A point about over-emphasis on content leads to suggestions that it is better to provide slimmed-down packages rather than create information overload. The advice is to concentrate on the building up and development of activities of multimedia resources and against learning programmes that over-direct students and leave nothing for students to demonstrate their diversity, creativity and originality. This would avoid the issue of 'uncritical contentment' (Evans 1987: 117), which has come to mean that perfectly written learning materials do not give students the opportunity to think further and there is nothing for the learner to interrogate.

Gibbs (1991) writes on student learning and provides practitioner-based experience on student-centred learning. Gibbs, when arguing for student-centred activities, talks about a hidden curriculum. He refers to a conventional approach where students are allowed to find for themselves or create an unofficial curriculum. The student-centred exercises were introduced to help students cope with the anxieties of study and with the organising and structuring of written work. One idea was the use of third-party accounts as a learning device. The task is for students to evaluate a piece of text dialogue. In the example offered, the third-party account was of a student telling other learners why she attended tutorials, and the question that followed was to ask the learner to write down and evaluate how effectively she conducted herself in the tutorial.

Resources that have a carefully structured route for learners are often organised from a user-centred perspective. Taylor et al. (1997) provide advice on the learner-centred approach to making resources with rich-media content, using The Galapagos Pilot Project as a case study for analysing learning behaviour. The project, a multimedia package in four episodes with learning tasks, was designed to help learners develop learning skills and decision-making processes. The framework that helped the design of the package supported learners as they worked their way through tasks prior to starting the process of reflection. The idea of giving control to users and creating tool and affordances for independent learning were judged to have worked, but only on the basis that the link between design semantics and task syntax could be interpreted by confident users. The less confident learners needed to follow a narrative line or thread running through each of the four episodes. The 'doing' part of the package is characterised by more exploratory activity. The structure allowed for the pages to be organised in a linear fashion during what the developers and creators refer to as the 'looking' session. At the end of the looking session there was a small amount of branching at which point the user would finish the episode and use a series of tools to tackle tasks for the 'doing' part.

Chen (2002) has added to this argument. There have been studies of non-linear learning programmes that have indicated that the features of these systems do not always benefit the learner. Evaluations have shown that there is a need to match the hypermedia learning system to individual learning needs, individual cognitive styles and learners' ability to restructure information.

This reintroduces the notion of the 'guidance seeker'. Bates's study of British Open University use of television and learning behaviour (1983) reaffirms the kind of learning behaviour that can thwart the good intentions of those developing rich-media learning materials for active learners. It reiterates the problems of weak learners using multimedia systems. Chen (2002) introduces us to the 'field dependent learner' and the 'field independent learner'. The former tended to take a passive approach requiring 'fixed paths' because they prefer to be guided in their learning process and be given conceptual descriptions for the possible sequences. The latter tend to take an active approach and are able to extract the relevant cues necessary for completion of a task.

Spiro and Jenhg (1990) discuss at great length an interactive computer programme containing a vast amount of video clips from the classic film *Citizen Kane*. It encouraged a self-initiated exploration of the thematic structures of the film. The authors discuss the 'potency' of dozens of experiences or mini-cases created out of real scenes from the film. It is a case-centred approach whereupon the authors avoided the use of a 'monolithic unit' because it was harder for learners to pull apart, and, hence, the programme uses very short pieces from larger scenes. The intention is for students to study the mini-cases independently. Then the students 'additively' reassembled the pieces as the whole case from separately considered conceptual parts' (Spiro and Jenhg 1990: 182). These mini-cases also promoted the idea of woven interconnectedness. The learners would see many examples of rich case analysis, the mini-case study could be used more than once, and it was easier to make connections between a small part of one case and a small part of another.

Let us consider in this next section the term experiential learning or a 'doing' approach to learning where learning takes the form of the capture of real life experiences. In this instance the learner is faced with the added challenge of working with media and media tools to create learning resources. The learner works as a producer of knowledge through the medium of audio or video and, in so doing, the learner or 'doer' has to reflect on what the 'doing' has achieved and to reflect on the interactions and processes that have been experienced. The value of rich media can be analysed further by reviewing Dale's cone of learning experiences (Dale 1969) and the art and craft of designing a piece of learning content from real events. The act of 'doing', analysing, reflecting which is then further incorporated and enhanced by designing, storyboarding in a rich media setting is an extension of the human experience of being in the real world. A multimedia application can have the affect of combining an interaction with the environment. The tools to aid interaction and online group work such as blogs and wikis are to affect the potential support that students can get from each other and that blogs and wikis can aid peer-to-peer communication and learning.

In the case study below, the authors of the research asked the students to work collaboratively with audio (Chan et al. 2006). The authors of this work have made a study of a podcasting approach to learning centred around three- to five-minute talkback radio-style 'shows' in which two or more students participate in informal discussions on pertinent issues relating to the course materials. There is minimal intervention from the lecturer, but, in establishing this, the process was made up of 'practice runs' and dialogue between the students prior to creating the learning object. This activity was not merely about making a recording, but actively scripting, storyboarding and designing linear content in a participatory way. The term 'ownership' typifies the way in which members would take responsibility for research, distribution and content writing.

Collis and Peters (1999) developed the concept of an experiential approach to making resources as opposed to learning from them. The student in this situation is converted from consumer to producer, and the video resource is placed in a database for access and reuse, therefore bringing student participation into the act of making resources.

If we shift our ideas from the traditional view of learning resources produced by practitioners and subject experts to one where technology is available for self-publication, we have the conditions to allow the learner access to rich media presentational tools for learning. If the topic can be handled in a way that the learner is able to discriminate between 'junk' information and quality information, to judge reliability and bias and to avoid distortion and sensationalism, the act of making resources is very similar to those students who build wikis or blogs. Sherry (1996) makes a brief reference to learners as active participants in the learning process. Students affect the manner in which they are dealing with materials. Learners must have a sense of ownership of the learning goals (Savery and Duffy 1995). They must be both willing and able to receive instructional messages and make something meaningful out of the materials presented. However, in situated learning, whereby learners take responsibility for learning, rich media learning resources and the tools to encourage the sharing and reuse of learning materials, is part of an active 'making' process that requires a number of cognitive, evaluative and reflective decision-making processes.

Conclusion

This chapter has emphasised the difficulties that educationists have in attempting to create a real-world experience through rich media. Video is good at conveying the teacher's ideas and the dominance of traditional teacher methods over many decades coupled with the use of rich media to express the teachers constructed view of the world is obviously a teacher-centred approach; the shift away from this is to create a more learner-centred approach. The narrative aspects of video have been discussed and clearly at some point in the development of video resources, there would have been an over reliance on a narrative structure to help learners build understanding of a topic. At one time (and sometimes it is still the case) that the learner played the role of a listener/watcher and the teacher played the role of storyteller. If the medium carries a complex structure it may undermine the learner's efforts to extract meaning and the active learning approach suffers. It is often the weaker learners that gain most from rich media, but only if the pace, delivery, media preference and narrative structure is presented in a way or form that is suitable for their learning style. The use of video, television and radio was not always considered an active learning experience unless the learner was able to use the media resource to reflect on an actual personal experience. In both linear and non-linear forms the experience is now being preceded by an activity that encourages interaction and one that Laurillard (1995) carefully defines as guided discovery. The learner gains control over the resource and the teacher's role in a multimedia application is one of tutorial support, stimulating learning rather than transmitting knowledge. Learners are involved in the learning process by having their interpretations of a real world event dealt with by a piece of software that assesses the learner's understanding through a set of 'activities' or tasks; the learner does not receive any expert answers or feedback until some learning is attempted. According to Mayer (2005) if the event or experience leads to behaviourism or behaviourist activity it is not active learning; cognitive activity is considered to be active learning whereupon the learner is looking to fill the gaps of his/her knowledge through reflection and through interrogation of the materials or the data being presented. It is important that advice given by Laurillard (1995) that breaking up chunks of linear media to create a multimedia package does not equate to guided discovery and that breaking a structure up into smaller sections can lead to fragmented knowledge. A final part of the conclusion is the instance where the learner becomes a producer of video or audio learning resources (Chan et al. 2006) and so by undertaking this role they become the active learner; someone who is researcher, writer, narrator, recorder and editor and in effect processing and reprocessing information to create knowledge. The study of children in a school (Feuerstein 1999) where media literacy lessons were given as an opportunity to develop critical thinking skills was shown that the added value of practical tools to make media increased the learning experience and aided critical thinking skills. The combination of these experiences, such as working with media to develop independent learning skills and being afforded the opportunity to view and evaluate rich media materials suggest that the role of rich media in active learning is very effective.

References

Bates, A. (1983) 'Adult Learning from Educational Television: The Open University Experience', in M. Howe (ed.), *Learning from Television Psychological and Educational Research,* London: Academic Press, pp. 57–76.

Bates, A. (1987) 'Educational Television Programme Structure and Style', available online at http://www.aber.ac.uk/media/Modules/TF33120/tvstyle.html. (Accessed 12 February 2004.)

Bates, A. (2005) *Technology, E-Learning and Distance Education,* London: Routledge.

Beard, C. and Wilson, J. (2001) *The Power of Experiential Learning,* London: Kogan Page.

Cennamo, K. (1993) 'Learning from Video: Factors Influencing Learners' Preconceptions and Invested Mental Effort', *Educational Technology Research and Development,* 41 (3): 33–45.

Chan, A., Lee, M., McLoughlin, C. (2006) 'Knowledge Creation Processes of Students as Producers of Audio Learning Objects', Part 3 Paper 1145, ALT 2007 conference research proceedings.

Chen, S. (2002) 'A Cognitive Model for Non-Linear Learning in Hypermedia Programmes', *British Journal of Educational Technology,* 33 (4): 449–60.

Clarke, A. (2001) *Designing Computer-Based Learning Materials,* Aldershot: Gower.

Collis, B. and Davies G. (eds) (1995) *Innovative Adult Learning with Innovative Technologies,* Amsterdam: Elsevier.

Collis, B. and Peters, O. (1999) 'At the Frontier: Asynchronous Video and the WWW for New Forms of Learning', in M. Moreau (ed.), *Distance Education at the Dawn of the Third Millennium,* Futuroscope, France: CNED, pp. 269–88.

Dale, Edgar (1969) *Audiovisual Methods in Teaching,* 3rd edn, New York: Holt/Dryden Publications.

Evans, N. (1987) *Assessing Experiential Learning: A Review of Progress and Practice,* London: Longman FEU.

Fallows, S. and Bhanot, R. (2002) *Educational Development through Information and Communications Technology,* London: SEDA Staff and Educational Development Series.

Feuerstein, M. (1999) 'Media Literacy in Support of Critical Thinking', *Journal of Educational Media,* 24 (1): 43–54.

Gibbs, G. (1991) *Teaching Students to Learn: A Student Centred Approach,* Buckingham: The Open University Press.

Laurillard, D. (1995) 'Multimedia and the Changing Experience of the Learner', *British Journal of Educational Technology,* 26 (3): 179–89.

Laurillard, D. (2002) *Rethinking University Teaching: A Conversational Framework for the Effective Use of Educational Technologies,* London and New York: RoutledgeFalmer.

Lockwood, F. (1992) *Activities in Self Instructional Texts,* London: Kogan Page.

Mayer, R. (2005) 'Introduction to Multimedia Learning', in R. E. Mayer (ed.), *The Cambridge Handbook of Educational Multimedia*, Cambridge: Cambridge University Press, pp. 1–16.

McFarland, D. (1996) 'Multimedia in Higher Education', available at http://www.lis.uiuc.edu/review/summer1996/mcfarland.html. (Accessed 18 November 2004.)

Race, P. (1996) 'Helping Students to Learn from Resources', in S. Brown and B. Smith (eds), *Resource Based Learning,* London: Kogan Page, pp. 26–36.

Salomon, G. (1984) 'Television is "Easy" and Print is "Tough": The Differential Investment of Mental Effort in Learning as a Function of Perceptions and Attributions', *Journal of Educational Psychology,* 76 (4): 647–58.

Savery, J. R. and Duffy, T. M. (1995) 'Problem Based Learning: an Instructional Model and Its Constructivist Framework', *Educational Technology,* 35 (5): 31–8.

Sherry, L. (1996) 'Issues in Distance Learning', *International Journal of Educational Telecommunications,* 1 (4): 337–65.

Spencer, K. (1988) *The Psychology of Educational Technology and Instructional Media,* London and New York: Routledge.

Spiro, R. J. and Jehng, J.-C. (1990) 'Cognitive Flexibility and Hypertext: Theory and Technology for the Nonlinear and Multidimensional Traversal of Complex Subject Matter', in D. Nix and R. Spiro (eds), *Cognition, Education and Multimedia: Exploring Ideas in High Technology,* Hillsdale, NJ: Lawrence Erlbaum Associates, pp. 163–207.

Taylor, J., Sumner, T. and Law, A. (1997) 'Talking About Multimedia: A Layered Design Framework', *Journal of Educational Media,* 23 (2/3): 215–41.

Chapter 4

Online Learning Issues for Active Citizenship

Karl Donert

The Internet makes huge amounts of information available to learners. Today's powerful information technologies also have the potential to promote a highly interactive computer-based approach to learning in higher education. The ability of computers to interface with learners has placed technology at the forefront of change in education. Computers are also very influential tools that provide the potential to individualise learning by creating flexible support systems for the many different types of learners (Kay 1998). So there has been an enormous growth in the use of the Internet and in the generation of multimedia resources. This has opened up new means of delivering university courses and course materials (Wang 2007).

There are a number of prevailing technological currents transforming society, producing different kinds of students, who expect diverse approaches to be delivered for their learning needs. These digital natives and digital immigrants are already engaging in an information society coupled with an online community culture that allows global interconnections to be easily made (Prensky 2001). Establishing learning that helps generate global citizens is vitally important.

In 1997, The Dearing Report (National Committee of Inquiry into Higher Education [NCIHE] 1997) published its review of the British higher-education system. It proposed underpinning principles of lifelong learning and inclusion with the utilisation of new technologies to establish a wider participation in universities. In order to deliver these objectives and to meet the challenges identified, the report confirmed that university courses would have to become more learner-centred, more open and flexible. This chapter thus reviews the types of knowledge environments which are likely to be needed to meet the challenges to establish active learners and active citizens. It also examines some of the issues associated with using relevant educational structures, tools and resources.

University Studies and Computer-Based Learning

For more than twenty years the use of computer-based learning (CBL) has been an integral part of higher education. CBL offers a powerful learning setting that can be used to enhance education in all subject areas. The computer technologies in use and the expectations may have changed since this time, but the needs and requirements of most university courses have not. The study of different educational contexts led Young (1990) to comment on three domains of knowledge: work knowledge, practical knowledge and emancipatory knowledge. Work knowledge referred to the way in which a student can control and manipulate their own learning space or environment; practical knowledge relates to human social interaction or communicative action; and the emancipatory domain identifies the use of self-knowledge and self-reflection. Such initial research has since led to the identification of a number of applicable computer-based learning methods which include collaborative learning, cooperative learning, discovery-based learning, engaged learning and problem-based learning.

Higher-education institutions have been undergoing significant changes, not only in their size and structure but also in their approaches to education and technological innovations (Jacobs and van der Ploeg 2005). They are all expected to include new information and communication technologies (ICT) as part of the educational approaches they offer.

Learning mediated by ICT is therefore becoming an important component of university studies because it enables and supports widening participation and provides inclusive educational opportunities. However, computer technologies also have the potential to transform education by generating innovative learning and teaching situations. Advances in ICT provide considerable opportunities to support learners as and when they need it and from any possible location. There remain three types of challenge facing CBL: learning and teaching challenges, organisational challenges and assessment challenges. The key to CBL success is in establishing how these barriers might be overcome and an adequate level of support offered

Higher-education programmes should respond to student needs. Specifically, they should provide appropriate courses with high-quality resources that suit their learning styles. Using innovative approaches with ICT will influence the attitudes of students and their motivation to learn, which will in turn affect their learning outcomes and result in increased retention. However, despite many initiatives, higher education remains relatively resistant to the wholesale adoption of new educational technologies. Collis and van der Wende (2002) investigated the choices that European higher education had made concerning the use of ICT. Their research showed that there have been few deep-seated changes in higher-education institutions, and, as a result, they did not expect major transformations to result from the use of ICT. They also showed that traditional delivery mechanisms remained the main approach used but that a form of blended learning widely existed using multiple strategies, delivery systems, tools and methods (Garrison and Kanuka 2004). In general, ICT was said to be embedded into learning and teaching in order to enhance courses.

E-Learning in UK Higher Education

E-Learning covers the many uses of ICT that higher-education institutions decide to adopt in their learning and teaching missions. There are many pressures driving the rise in use of e-learning within UK higher education (Higher Education Funding Council for England [HEFCE] 2005), with the primary strategic goal to help institutions and practitioners explore the possibilities of transforming the student learning experience.

Most universities have invested in learning community software, often referred to as virtual learning environments (VLEs) to deliver learning content and activities to their students. This software often consists of a core set of features which include the delivery of learning materials, learner administration functions such as progress tracking, assessment, different forms of communications, planning, organisation and timetabling facilities, searching tools and online help (Singh et al. 2005). A VLE is thus used to act as a focus for students' learning activities and the management and facilitation of learning support, along with the provision of content and resources required to help make the activities successful (Stiles 2000). VLEs then facilitate and enhance student learning through the numerous resources provided and activities they are asked to complete. The key function is that they are established to provide a framework for learners to manage their own learning. They thus provide realistic opportunities to encourage student-centred approaches. So the environments themselves do not enhance learning, it the ways in which they can be used that are significant.

Through all the hype there has been some scepticism raised concerning the value of online learning. Russell (2001) coined this as the 'no significant difference' phenomena, which suggests that negative images for online learning are promoted. Such cynicism often relates to the lack of quality and positive learning experiences provided by the courses and resources on offer. If this is to be redressed, there remains a need to provide high-quality resources together with challenging learning activities that will promote constructive educational aspects. In order to do this, e-learning needs to be more fully understood and accepted. Kirschner and Paas (2001) suggest that it appears as if higher-education institutions want to embrace the potential of educational support, administration and assessment that ICT brings. However, they commented that it is almost impossible to find real 'web-enhanced' education, as universities exhibit typically resistant behaviour towards the integrated penetration of modern technology in the learning process.

Conole (2002) contends that current developments of structured learning environments are occurring on the whole in parallel to the generation of huge numbers of accessible learning resources. There has also been an increasing sophistication of the online resources available. However, far from making things easier for learners, the technology can provide them with information overload, making it difficult for them to filter out irrelevant and inaccurate information, or else resulting in the dominance of biased viewpoints rather than balanced interpretations. To counter this, users will have to think critically about their information requirements in a specific context and then they will need to assess the relevance of the different online resources which are available to meet their needs.

So, there are strong implications that the use of VLEs is changing the way that some aspects of higher education have been and are being delivered. However, the effectiveness of VLEs for learning depends mostly on the abilities and competences of the learners and what pedagogic methods are being employed.

Computer Literacy

As computers have become more and more a part of modern-day life, with more homes than ever having access to personal computers, computer literacy or the knowledge and ability to use computers and related technology efficiently is at an all time high. Computer literacy is therefore what all students would need in order for them to be informed citizens, to compete in the job market and to be able to function within society. In order to be computer literate, people also need to understand what computers can and cannot do, when to use them and when to avoid them, and how our use of computers affects us and those around us.

Olsen (1996) takes computer literacy one step further, linking it with thinking, so that it involves engagement in a dialogue that will allow learners to reflect on the words and phrases used and thus they become more reflective and analytical. In this way, using the course materials presented through the Active Learning/Active Citizenship project (ALAC) should require students to demonstrate computer literacy in its broader sense. Not only does access to resources and materials occur online, but it is also important in encouraging engagement with the resources and other students. Tutors will thus be expecting students to be able to display a high level of computer literacy; however, this is something perhaps that higher education might be taking for granted.

There is widespread acceptance of the need for ICT literacy among university students. Wecker et al. (2007), for example, investigated the role of computer learning as a learning prerequisite for knowledge acquisition, and they analyse the learner patterns of media use and how they are related to processing strategies and procedural computer-related knowledge. There appears, however, to be relatively little UK information available that helps higher-education organisations assist learners to identify ICT gaps in their learning requirements or what might be done to address them. This has been remedied in the case of teacher training in England and Wales, where an ICT skills test forms a compulsory part of the training profile required if graduates are to achieve qualified teacher status. The test is intended to ensure that everyone qualifying to teach has a good grounding in the use of ICT in the wider context of their professional role as a teacher (Training and Development Agency 2007). In the USA, the Educational Testing Service (2007) recently proposed ICT as a core competency for university students. They commented that there is an urgent need for higher education to focus on the information proficiency divide and to evaluate the effectiveness of efforts taken to improve the ICT skills that students need if they are to be successful in an information-rich, technology-based society. They identified a series of seven ICT proficiencies to help improve the effectiveness of teaching strategies and curricula, to identify best practices and to initiate better approaches (see Table 4.1). These components are likely to need to become an important part of the personal development needs for lifelong learning (Rockman and Smith 2005).

Proficiency	Definition
Define	Using ICT tools to identify and appropriately represent an information need.
Access	Collecting and/or retrieving information in digital environments.
Manage	Using ICT tools to apply an existing organizational or classification scheme for information.
Integrate	Interpreting and representing information, such as by using ICT tools to synthesise, summarise, compare, and contrast information from multiple sources.
Evaluate	Judging the degree to which information satisfies the needs of the task in ICT environments, including determining authority, bias, and timeliness of materials.
Create	Adapting, applying, designing, or inventing information in ICT environments.
Communicate	Communicating information properly in its context (audience, media) in ICT environments.

Table 4.1 Components of ICT literacy.

Note: ICT Literacy as defined on page 18 of the Educational Testing Service's report, *Succeeding in the 21st Century: What Higher Education Must Do to Address the Gap in Information and Communication Technology Proficiencies*. Available online at:

<http://www.ets.org/Media/Tests/Information_and_Communication_Te chnology_Literacy/ICTwhitepaperfinal.pdf>

Active Citizenship in Education

Until recently, the concept of citizenship was commonly understood in rather static and institutionally dominated terms through legal entitlements and their political expression (European Commission 2000). There are also many definitions of citizenship in education, most of which relate to the extension of knowledge, skills, attitudes and values to stimulate participation in the democratic and cultural processes of identity. Active citizenship in education focuses on the relationships between the individual and society usually in terms of the legal, social, economic, cultural and technological dimensions, resulting in respect, interest in community affairs, responsibility and participation (Campaign for Real Education 1999; Kerr 1999).

In schools, citizenship became a new statutory foundation subject at Key Stages 3 and 4 in 2002 (Donert, in press). It was recognised by those involved in implementing this policy that if citizenship education was to be developed effectively, then schools would need additional support through the provision of suitable resources. Therefore, a mapping exercise was undertaken of the resources for schools that were available, or were in preparation (Kerr et al. 2000). Over 300 resources were identified and catalogued, and, from this, they identified that there was a general shortage of resources. The situation was especially weak in coverage of certain topic areas such as democracy and that there was poor coverage of certain skills, such as participation in school councils, political literacy and democratic skills. The mapping exercise recommended that education should receive necessary support to raise awareness, to regularly update the resource map and to disseminate the findings. This research allowed subject organisations, non-governmental organisations and other interested agencies to focus their resource development in areas that needed it most.

Cullingford (2000) comments on the complexity of citizenship as an academic subject, when it is related closely to attitudes at home, to neighbourhoods and communities and to groups and society. Andrews and Lewis (2002) analyse the ideas inherent in citizenship curricula through four components of citizenship: active citizenship, cultural citizenship, global citizenship and comprehensive citizenship involving all the other actions. Active citizenship, they suggest, is based on engagement and participation which is associated with obligations and responsibilities. The concept of cultural citizenship focuses upon a sense of belonging and tradition, global citizenship is usually addressed through awareness of the wider impact of human activities on our society, and comprehensive citizenship results in a much deeper approach as it implies a combined and profound approach to being a citizen which should lead to the development of a sense of responsibility and the desire to 'make a difference'.

The idea of teaching active citizenship is clearly attractive, but it needs to be adequately supported by a broad range of teaching and learning approaches based on quality resources with structured opportunities for students to be actively involved in discussion and debate on topical and contemporary issues (Janoski 1998) and through case studies, projects and activities in the local community. To help young people to understand each other and to collaborate, to be tolerant and full of curiosity about the world around them is not something that can be argued against. The application of ICT offers learners a high degree of relevance in academic study because its use significantly influences the construction of new ways of life and modern economic, social and cultural approaches. The question which arises is whether ICT can be used in building active citizenship education, and, if so, what approaches can and should be used to maximise its effectiveness?

What Kinds of ICT for Delivering Active-Citizenship Education?

University students using ICT to find out information for assignments are being active learners, engaging in and identifying problems and then attempting to solve them by finding relevant information from various sources, critically evaluating and then analysing it. However, they may not necessarily engage by means of empathy with the issues concerned.

Research on the impact of student-centred methods combined with the use of ICT tools indicates that ICT tools are predominantly used by students for information seeking (Alexandersson and Limberg 2005). But the potential role of ICT is far broader than this as it should also be used to help gather and catalogue information, to transform and reproduce information, to enable channels for collaboration about information, to present information and to communicate information beyond the local to a global scale.

Using ICT for learning also encourages a strongly student-centred rather than teacher-centred approach. ICT can therefore contribute to active citizenship education by providing a wide range of information sources, which will encourage students to become critically aware of issues. ICT also has the potential to help them develop an understanding of the complex interrelationships between people and their activities and in exchanging information and opinions via communications. The tools and resources therefore should provide flexibility and autonomy while enabling creativity, imagination and critical thinking (Donert 2002).

There are three main areas where ICT can provide significant benefits to citizenship education: exploration and information-gathering, experimentation and reflection, and collaboration and communications. Through exploration and information-gathering the relationship between students, information and knowledge is changing. Many students are active in online information communities and therefore most of them already have access to a wide variety of digital information sources. The combined use of different media allows the development of a multi-sensory approach to studying. However, learning can not only be enhanced by enabling access to materials but also in preparing and sharing authentic information and materials with others. The obvious pedagogical benefits associated with the process include pride in presentation, ownership of information, sharing, social interaction and sense of purpose through active engagement.

Experimentation and reflection helps learning take place through ICT. These approaches play a crucial role in enabling students to become constructive, creative learners through the use of available resources. However, access to information does not help learners to understand the complexity and dynamics of a given situation, nor will it allow them to interpret their attitudes to generate opinions and decide on possible actions. Young people need to be encouraged to develop a deeper understanding and sense of citizenship. Most students rarely had the opportunity to develop critical thinking while at school. They have often been protected and even excluded from decision-making and in developing attitudes and values. The use of ICT can provide a liberating influence by providing tools and resources that will help learners to consider, review and reflect on, so that they might be able to understand and interpret complex situations. A combination of ICT tools that will allow learners to experiment and reflect would be important to support these activities. These tools might include:

- modelling, simulation and scenario-building to help interpretation and understanding of causal links and factors;
- cybervenues for individual and collective reflection;
- systems that will encourage action planning, the critical skills of analysis with a view to decision-making.

The likely outcomes if this approach was adopted would be a series of suitable learning tasks that would require students to consider the complexity of the content under consideration in order to engage them in higher-order cognitive processes, such as synthesis, analysis, restructuring of information and ideas, reflection and evaluation.

Using collaborative approaches provides opportunities to use ICT as a communications tool to support learners. Participatory technologies such as email and mobile phones are increasingly providing individualised communications, yet they also offer great potential for active collaboration. They can be used to give support, enable interaction and cooperation and even provide access to experts. New communication technologies have also become an integral part of the socialisation process for young people who are influenced greatly by media and seem to be deeply affected by and interested in issues that concern them.

There are three important ICT components for tutors to consider when developing active citizenship education. These are enabling access to relevant, challenging and suitable resources, providing learners with support and guidance and promoting peer dialogue through communication, discussion, reflection and review.

Effective active learning involves individual activities and those that are undertaken as part of communities or groups of learners. Individual learning can be defined as the capacity to build knowledge through individual reflection about external stimuli and sources, and through the personal re-elaboration of individual knowledge and experience in light of interaction with others and the learning environment (Tait and Knight 1996). This involves being more active through interactions leading to the type of active learning that provides opportunities for students to devise their own questions, discuss issues, explain their own opinions and engage in cooperative learning by working in teams on problems and projects. This can be enhanced by online forms of communication. Activity theory has been used to emphasise social factors in learning and the interaction between learners and their learning environments. It seeks to explain how the tools and resources provided shape the way learners interact with the learning system (Kuutti 1995). The learner experience can be accumulated in the properties and content of the materials as well as how they should be used. This human–computer interaction has gained a reputation as one of the central elements in designing for active learning.

Cook (2002) examined the role of dialogue in learning. For many students, the amount and types of personal contact that take place during an academic course is very important. As ICT is increasingly used in university studies, this should allow an increase in the level of communication between peer learners and also with tutors. However, effective dialogue can only be the case if both synchronous and asynchronous communication tools are used and effective communication channels are established through online and face-to-face opportunities where possible.

ICT resources and online media repositories do not normally provide guidance on how they should be integrated and embedded in a coherent fashion so that effective learning can occur. Establishing dialogue may be required, for example, if the goal is to promote reflection and conceptual change. Dialogue enables the student to verbalise and articulate his or her needs and understandings. Mercer (2000) suggests breaking down dialogue into disputational, cumulative and exploratory components to understand the process better. McDermott (1999) argues that we learn through interaction with others, and, given the opportunity, we quickly spread that knowledge. Sometimes this learning effect through dialogue has been called 'scaffolding' (Sharma and Hannafin 2007).

Some learners thrive in group situations and benefit immensely from being able to collaborate with others. Group study improves students intellectually. When done effectively, it stimulates their interest and increases confidence. Group study involves:

- sharing of ideas, personal and collective time management, and task preparation;
- cooperation amongst group members;
- collective responsibility both for the group task and for each other's welfare;
- a willingness to be an active group participant.

In group work, students can build on each other's strengths.

Modern approaches to learning and teaching usually encourage significant student interaction and discussion. Graff (2006) suggests that interaction between learners in their courses could be of great importance to learner success. Current research suggests this peer interaction is conducive to learning and understanding. Holmes and Gardner (2006), for example, comment that the contributions made by individuals when working towards common goals are some of the most powerful factors in promoting learning. Gregory and Chapman (2006), however, suggest that groups work best when they have no more than four students. Managing and supporting peer learning should thus be a high priority for course development in ALAC.

Most undergraduate students today will have participated for many years in informal online communities such as MySpace and Friends Reunited. Nevertheless, many of them do not find it easy to be active participants in online academic discussion and debate. Students who are not engaged in participating online have been described by Perkins and Newman (1996) as lurkers. They are described as the silent majority who engage but are not active in an electronic forum. Nonnecke and Preece (2000a) suggest that lurkers may make up over 90 per cent of most online groups. This may be because they are uncomfortable with expressing their views or intimidated by the expertise or eloquence of the participants (Preece and Nonnecke 2001).

Establishing active learners in higher education implies that approaches have to be sought to encourage all learner types to engage, connect, participate and contribute online (Klemm 1998; Salmon 2000). Lurkers can annoy some participants but all those involved need to be understanding and accept that this is simply a natural response for many students. So, tutors should be aware that lurking is normal and that everyone lurks sometime (Nonnecke and Preece 2000b). Thus, while lurking may be perceived to be a problem, it probably is not as long as all the students concerned are engaged in active thinking processes (Preece et al. 2004).

Design for Active Citizenship

Two design components should be considered for active citizenship: first, there are some technical aspects which should be considered and in particular the usability of the ALAC materials and website, and, second, attention should be paid to the ways in which the technologies used might be able to help create a pedagogical design process that will encourage active learning for active citizenship.

Usability is paramount for the success of any resources and websites available on the Internet. Usability relates to the question of how well users can exploit the functionality of the materials available (Costabile and Matera 2001). Lynch (1995) confirms that it is important to make sure there is a balance between all the elements that make a website to ensure that it is usable. A balance in the structure of the menu interface, information-based content, graphics and any other forms of multimedia. When this is achieved, the site can then be built with a hierarchical structure which feels natural to the user and which flows more easily. In this way, usability is closely related to digital literacy so that information in multiple formats from a wide range of sources can be used. Conole (2002) comments on the associated usability and navigational issues that result in a range of strategies which can be used to manage online information and to provide different searching protocols, navigational aids and maps. Earle (2002) describes flexibility and customisability as significant design criterion at the heart of educational learning systems for higher education. The result will be the creation of dominantly learner-centred approaches which will help students to become independent, lifelong learners. This significantly changes the role of the tutor who becomes a mentor-adviser and catalyst of learning.

As in most learning situations, students are usually more engaged when they face a challenge that they feel they can meet. The level of the challenge presented should therefore match the potential ability of the students. If the task is too hard, the student will give up easily, and, if it is too easy, the student may become bored. Students also need to reflect and be challenged so that they will benefit from active approaches. For example, the use of scenario-building encourages critical thought and the analysis of complexity. Undergraduate learners ought to be able to handle this if they are supported effectively by including opportunities and tools for students to reflect on and explain what is happening. In fact, in multifaceted situations, learning may not occur without such guidance and significant time for reflection. Students may also become caught up in the problem and not deal with the learning. In this case, pedagogical tools will be required to help them reflect on what they are learning by providing explanations and questions for them to answer.

Henderson (1996) suggested some fundamental web-design principles which should result in constructive, authentic, flexible and supportive activities that will allow self-direction, cooperation, collaboration and multiple perspectives to be considered. Structured learning scenarios that can be explored by the learners' required component resources to be available in a flexible format to meet learner needs. As a result, a component-orientated problem-based process was likely to evolve on the ALAC website around the core citizenship competences of awareness, information, understanding, involvement and responsible action. It should in different situations be possible to map these against ICT opportunities as illustrated in Table 4.2:

ALAC component	Description	Likely activity	Approach
Awareness	Describe the issue and its origin, consider activities	Create the context through discussion, reflection and review	Collective
Information	Collect and collate information from different aspects	Pool existing knowledge	Collaborative research

Analysis	Assess the issue in the light of the gathered information or lack of it	Process information in order to establish ideas, values, rights and opinions	Sharing
Understanding	Understand the situation concerned	Present and share information so that the process can be clarified and a suitable approach be adopted	Cooperation
Deliberation	Generate and consider different perspectives and points of view	Extract and problem-solve, communicate information	Reflective knowledge construction
Involvement	Decide on a particular standpoint, provide the arguments for and against it	Present ideas and share, discuss and reach conclusions, consider complexity	Reflect and discuss
Responsible action	Devise action plan to meet objectives	Debrief, act on views and opinions	Produce and publish action

Table 4.2: Some ALAC pedagogical components.

Through establishing a clear pedagogical approach and sound organisational models, it is anticipated that clear learning approaches will be generated to establish effective engagement with the ALAC philosophy in an innovative, interactive, highly motivating and enjoyable way. Interactivity is a key feature of the use of ICT resources for learning, and, because of its interactive nature, learners should have access to information in whatever way suits their purpose or learning style. The predominance of multimedia learning opportunities are intended to enhance a deeper learning process by providing access to some of the complex messages involved. However, Mayer (2003) warns that it is the instructional method that promotes learning rather than the delivery device of the message, finding no media effects in situations where the same methods were used with books and computers.

Conclusions

As higher education grapples with integrating technology-orientated learner-support systems, current changes in online learning and teaching are predominantly being institution-led and then demand driven. The scholarly academic appears to have little real control over the process, except through the creation and use of high-quality Internet-based resources which can effectively support learning, teaching and assessment. If the majority of academic staff is to be successful in establishing active e-learning into their teaching, then the approaches in use must be meaningful to them on a personal level (Lawson and de Matos 2000). Unfortunately, much of higher education remains laggard in terms of its innovative and active uses of online learning characteristics. E-learning enthusiasts still remain largely isolated in their own institutional context. They seem to have little influence on the behaviour of others. The significance of a project such as ALAC in gathering and then testing ideas should therefore not be underestimated.

The role of ALAC should be to stimulate, encourage and support change. The outcomes, including the strategies employed for using innovative approaches in learning and teaching with technology, will need to be positively promoted by increasing awareness of the project and raising the profile of its achievements in providing a challenging student learning environment for active learning and active citizenship (Osler and Vincent 2002). Rogers (1995) comments on the importance of observability and trialability when seeking to innovate and then disseminate successful outcomes. Observability is the degree to which the results are visible to others, and trialability seeks to promote a culture of inquiry so that widespread dissemination through positive promotion can be carried out with evidence from action research. Higher education has a lot to learn therefore from the ALAC project where innovative practice has taken place.

It is likely that some of the results of the ALAC project will suggest that both active learning and active citizenship should be integrated into many courses across the sector and that all institutions should seek to offer the sorts of online approaches to those developed through ALAC. Perhaps the greatest impact is likely to occur in situations where ICT can deliver user choice and learner independence with sufficient flexibility that allows learners themselves to manage their own learning and individualise their education process. Those institutions that may wish to do this will need considerable advice and guidance, more so in pedagogical terms than for technological aspects. So, the mission of ALAC should now be to provide a range of support materials for tutors who may wish to use the digital resources and ALAC website and to enable the creation and construction of an online professional community of ALAC academics, as envisaged by Howard Rheingold (1993), who consider active learning and active citizenship to be core components of undergraduate study. The establishment of the ALAC wiki (http://alac.pbwiki.com) is the first step in this process.

To summarise, ALAC examines some of educational changes associated with the construction of tomorrow's society. It will require academics to integrate challenging citizenship issues, multiple perspectives and trans-cultural interpretations into their teaching and student learning experiences. This can only be possible if their students have an opportunity to communicate, collaborate and be creative and reflective (Kezar 2005). This approach will encourage them to manage and be responsible for their own learning. It is clear that ICT can deliver freedom of choice and independence in space and time. But the impact of digital technologies on 'educated' young people, their values and perceptions and needs could be very significant.

The ALAC project has been designed to encourage the meaningful integration of ICT into the learning processes for active citizenship in a number of undergraduate degree courses. As such, the materials and resources that have been created impact significantly on the development of young people, while transforming many of the pedagogical practices implemented by their mentors and the other academics involved. ALAC therefore provides opportunities for course tutors to generate flexibility in the learning process of their students. It is hoped that the project outcomes will lead to variety in the learning situations that are implemented, allowing all those involved to grasp the changing dynamics of learning about citizenship using ICT and to establish the learning experiences that they all need to be global citizens.

References

Alexandersson, M. and Limberg, L. (2005) 'In the Shade of the Knowledge Society and the Importance of Information Literacy', paper presented at the 11th Biennial Earli Conference, University of Cyprus, Nicosia, Cyprus, 23–7 August.

Andrews, D. and Lewis, M. (2002) 'The Experience of a Professional Community: Teachers Developing a New Image of Themselves and Their Workplace', *Educational Research,* 44 (3): 237–54.

Campaign for Real Education (1999) *Critique of Education for Citizenship and the Teaching of Democracy in Schools: Final Report of the Advisory Group on Citizenship,* London: Qualifications and Curriculum Authority.

Collis, B. and van der Wende, M. (2002) *Models of Technology and Change in Higher Education: an International Comparative Survey on the Current and Future Use of ICT in Higher Education,* Enschede: Centre for Higher Education Policy Studies.

Conole, G. (2002) 'Systematising Learning and Research Information', *Journal of Interactive Media in Education,* available online at http://www-jime.open.ac.uk/2002/7 (accessed 22 December 2007).

Cook, J. (2002) 'The Role of Dialogue in Computer-Based Learning and Observing Learning: an Evolutionary Approach to Theory', *Journal of Interactive Media in Education,* 5, available online at http://www-jime.open.ac.uk/2002/5. (Accessed 22 December 2007.)

Costabile, M. F. and Matera, M. (2001) 'Guidelines for Hypermedia Usability Inspection', *IEEE MultiMedia,* 8 (1): 66–9.

Cullingford, C. (2000) 'Citizenship and Nationality: How Young People Develop Prejudice', paper presented at the European Conference on Educational Research, Edinburgh, 20–3 September.

Donert, K. (2002) 'European Citizenship: A New Educational Focus: Some Opportunities for ODL', Proc. EDEN 11th anniversary conference, Granada: European Distance Education Network, pp. 441–60.

—— (in press) 'Examining the Relationship Between Citizenship and Geography', in N. Labrinos (ed.), *School Geography in Europe,* Washington, DC: National Council for Geographic Education.

Earle, A. (2002) 'Designing for Pedagogical Flexibility: Experiences from the CANDLE Project', *Journal of Interactive Media in Education,* available online at http://www-jime.open.ac.uk/2002/4. (Accessed 22 December 2007.)

Educational Testing Service (2007) *Succeeding in the 21st Century: What Higher Education Must Do to Address the Gap in Information and Communication Technology Proficiencies,* Princeton, NJ: Educational Testing Service.

European Commission (2000) 'Learning for Active Citizenship: A Significant Challenge in Building a Europe of Knowledge', available online at http://europa.eu.int/comm/education/citizen/citiz-en.html. (Accessed 14 July 2005.)

Garrison, D. R. and Kanuka, H. (2004) 'Blended Learning: Uncovering Its Transformative Potential in Higher Education', *The Internet and Higher Education,* 7 (2): 95–105.

Graff, M. (2006) 'The Importance of Online Community in Student Academic Performance', *Electronic Journal of e-learning,* 4 (2): 127–32.

Gregory, G. and Chapman, C. (2006) *Differentiated Instructional Strategies: One Size Doesn't Fit All,* Thousand Oaks, Calif.: Corwin Press.

Higher Education Funding Council for England (2005) HEFCE Strategy for E-Learning, Bristol: Higher Education Funding Council for England.

Henderson, L. (1996) 'Instructional Design of Interactive Multimedia', *Educational Technology Research and Development,* 44 (4): 85–104.

Holmes, B. and Gardner, J. (2006) *E-Learning Concepts and Practices,* London: Sage Publications.

Jacobs, B. and van der Ploeg, F. (2005) *Guide to Reform of Higher Education: A European Perspective,* London: CESifo and CEPR.

Janoski, T. (1998) *Citizenship and Civil Society: A Framework of Rights and Obligations in Liberal, Traditional, and Social Democratic Regimes,* Cambridge: Cambridge University Press.

Kay, A. C. (1998) 'Computers, Networks and Education', *Scientific American,* 265 (3): 100–7.

Kerr, D. (1999) *Citizenship Education: An International Comparison – International Review of Curriculum and Assessment Frameworks,* London: QCA.

Kerr, D., Blenkinsop, S. and Dartnall, L. (2000) 'Review of Citizenship Education Resources', available online at http://www.nfer.ac.uk/research-areas/pims-data/summaries/rce-review-of-citizenship-education-resources.cfm (accessed 1 February 2006).

Kezar, A. (2005) 'Redesigning for Collaboration Within Higher Education Institutions: An Exploration into the Developmental Process', *Research in Higher Education,* 46 (7): 831–60.

Kirschner, P. A. and Paas, F. (2001) 'Web-Enhanced Higher Education: A Tower of Babel', *Computers in Human Behaviour,* 17 (4): 347–53.

Klemm, W. (1998) 'Eight Ways to Get Students More Engaged in Online Conferences', *THE Journal,* 26 (1): 62–4.

Kuutti, K. (1995) 'Activity Theory As a Potential Framework for Human-Computer Interaction Research', in B. Nardi (ed.), *Context and Consciousness: Activity Theory and Human Computer Interaction,* Cambridge, Mass.: MIT Press, pp. 17–44.

Lawson, R. and de Matos, C. (2000) 'Information Technology Skills in the Workplace: Implications for Bachelor of Arts Degrees', *Australian Journal of Educational Technology,* 16 (2): 87–103.

Lynch, P. J. (1995) 'Yale University Web Style Guide', available online at http://www.webstyleguide.com/index.html?/contents.html. (Accessed 26 February 2009.)

McDermott, R. (1999) *Learning Across Teams: The Role of Communities of Practice in Team Organizations,* Boulder, Col.: Organization Memory and Organizational Learning Project, Center for LifeLong Learning and Design, University of Colorado.

Mayer, R. (2003) 'Elements of a Science of E-Learning', *Journal of Educational Computing Research,* 29 (3): 297–313.

Mercer, N. (2000) *Words and Minds: How We Use Language to Think Together,* London: Routledge.

National Committee of Inquiry into Higher Education (1997) *The Dearing Report: Higher Education in the Learning Society,* Hayes: National Committee of Inquiry into Higher Education.

Nonnecke, B. and Preece, J. W. L. L. (2000a) 'Lurker Demographics: Counting the Silent', paper presented at the Proceedings of CHI 2000, The Hague.

—— (2000b) 'Why Lurkers Lurk', paper presented at the AMCIS Conference, Boston, 1 June.

Olsen, D. (1996) *Modes of Thought: Explorations in Culture and Cognition,* Cambridge: Cambridge University Press.

Osler, A. and Vincent, K. (2002) *Citizenship and the Challenge of Global Education,* Stoke on Trent: Trentham.

Perkins, J. and Newman, K. (1996) 'Two Archetypes in E-Discourse: Lurkers and Virtuosos', *International Journal of Educational Telecommunications,* 2 (2): 155–70.

Preece, J. and Nonnecke, B. (2001) 'Why Lurkers Lurk', paper presented at the AMCIS Conference, Boston, June.

Preece, J., Nonnecke, B. and Andrews, D. (2004) 'The Top Five Reasons for Lurking: Improving Community Experiences for Everyone', *Computers in Human Behavior,* 2 (2): 201–23.

Prensky, M. (2001) 'Digital Natives, Digital Immigrants Part 2: Do They Really Think Differently?', *On The Horizon: The Strategic Planning Resource for Education Professionals,* 9 (6): 1–6.

Rheingold, H. (1993) *The Virtual Community: Homesteading on the Electronic Frontier,* Reading, Mass.: Addison-Wesley.

Rockman, I. F. and Smith, G. W. (2005) 'Information and Communication Technology Literacy: New Assessments for Higher Education', *College & Research Libraries News,* 66 (8): 587–9.

Rogers, E. M. (1995) *Diffusion of Innovations,* New York: The Free Press.

Salmon, G. (2000) *E-Moderating: The Key to Teaching and Learning Online,* 2nd edn, Abingdon: RoutledgeFalmer.

Sharma, P. and Hannafin, M. (2007) 'Scaffolding in Technology-Enhanced Learning Environments', *Interactive Learning Environments,* 15 (1): 27–46.

Singh, G., O'Donoghue, J. and Worton, H. (2005) 'A Study into the Effects of Elearning on Higher Education', *Journal of University Teaching and Learning Practice,* 2 (1), available online at http://jutlp.uow.edu.au/2005_vo2_io1/pdf/odonoghue_003.pdf. (Accessed 22 December 2007.)

Stiles, M. (2000) 'Effective Learning and the Virtual Environment', paper presented at the Proceedings: EUNIS 2000: Towards Virtual Universities, Instytut Informatyki Politechniki Poznanskiej, Poznan, April.

Tait, J. and Knight, P. (1996) *The Management of Independent Learning,* London: Kogan Page.

Training and Development Agency (TDA) (2007) 'ICT QTS Skills Test', available online at http://www.tda.gov.uk/skillstests/ict.aspx. (Accessed 23 December 2007.)

Wang, Y.-M. (2007) 'Internet Uses in University Courses', *International Journal on E-Learning,* 6 (2): 279–92.

Wecker, C., Kohnle, C. and Fischer, F. (2007) 'Computer Literacy and Inquiry Learning: When Geeks Learn Less', *Journal of Computer Assisted Learning,* 23 (2): 133–44.

Young, R. (1990) *A Critical Theory of Education: Habermas and Our Children's Future,* New York: Teachers' College Press.

Chapter 5

A Pedagogy of Connection for Active Learning and Citizenship

Patrick Dillon

The chapter is about connections between active learning and citizenship and ways in which the connections might be facilitated. It builds on an earlier paper where I made a case for a pedagogy of connection for engaging with complex and multifaceted issues. My argument was that we should integrate content between and across disciplines. I dealt with a pedagogy of connection at a general level, setting out some overarching principles about establishing the contexts of connection and developing tools for making the connections (Dillon 2006).

Inter- and multidisciplinary approaches are good for addressing complex issues that benefit from the integration of different forms of knowledge. But citizenship is as much about 'being' as it is about 'knowing': it defines a particular type of engagement with the world. In this chapter I will extend the pedagogy of connection to embrace sources of information, particularly sources that are developed externally to academia such as policy documents and their enactment through managerial structures and re-presentation through the media and journalism. For most people, these sources are the primary means through which they become informed about matters of citizenship. It is by struggling with the information, challenging it, internalising it, that opinions and beliefs are formed and actions justified. The information is thus both a resource for courses in higher education and a source of tension with the formal academic content of those courses. In this sense, the information may be regarded as a boundary object.

The term 'boundary object' was coined by Star and Griesemer (1989). They were working on an environmental and archival conservation project where transactions had to be brokered between different academic, professional, amateur and administrative actors to enable the project to be brought to fruition. From this specific derivation of the term, a more general conceptualisation has been developed. Boundary objects are now defined as artefacts, documents, institutional and administrative protocols and the like, which have to be addressed by people from different communities if shared understandings are to be built. A boundary has been defined by Walker and Creanor (2005) as a discontinuity in some form of practice, often determined by limits of effective communication. In what follows boundaries are between (i) communities of policy-makers, those enacting policy and those re-presenting policy, taken collectively, and communities of academics, and (ii) communities of academics and communities of students. Boundary encounters occur as people interact across these boundaries, interpersonally and through the mediation of information. Boundary crossings are the flow of ideas, constructs and innovations across the boundaries.

There are many ways to address citizenship, and in education it is a contested concept (Beck 1996). Education can be 'about', 'through' or 'for' citizenship. In order to provide a focus in this chapter, I adopt a perspective based on what might be regarded as some classical subject matter of citizenship, broadly corresponding to that described by Marshall (1950). I recognise that this subject matter is open to challenge. The purpose, however, is not to explore competing definitions of citizenship but, rather, to look at how a pedagogy of connection might be developed from a defined starting point. My concern then is with some key concepts that structure social, moral and political positions. They are:

- the structure of power;
- customary and alternative ways of taking decisions, settling disputes and allocating resources;

- the main political issues and disputes, who promotes what policies, goals and values and why they promote them;
- the nature and basis of duties, responsibilities, and rights and the roles of custom and law in prescribing them;
- fairness, justice and moral responsibility;
- similarities and differences between individuals, groups and communities and the nature of cooperation and competition between them;
- how communities reconcile the needs of individuals with the structure of society;
- respect for different ways of life, beliefs, opinions and ideas;
- consideration of moral dilemmas.

This content is implicit in the sources of information discussed below.

Outside of universities, students' exposure to issues of citizenship is fragmental, influenced to varying degrees by policy-making, management, the media, journalism and the World Wide Web. Through each of these boundary encounters, 'content' is subject to increasing selection, both overt and covert and becomes increasingly value-laden. Policy represents a political ideal, which in its implementation is constrained by managerial decisions based on legal, economic, social and, sometimes, moral imperatives. Journalism, in the way it assigns value, imposes further tiers of selection, reinterpretation and re-presentation. The most selective sources of information – newspapers, television and the World Wide Web – are the most readily available and widely utilised. On the one hand, engagement with these sources is a passive form of intellectual consumerism: 'interpretation' turns information into a leisure commodity through channelled engagement. On the other hand, the Internet and, to a lesser extent, the interactive features of television offer more proactive forms of engagement. Making connections between the works of those who generate, implement, report and re-present policy with those who construct academic interpretations around policy offers students the possibility of developing a more coherent understanding of citizenship and of clarifying their own values.

There are many tiers of policy-making. Policy is a statement of intent. The extent to which it becomes practice in a democracy depends on processes of government and the degree of enforcement of international and national law. Policy may arise from global imperatives. It may represent the interests of a number of nations acting collectively. The European Union, for example, sets standards that govern matters in its member states. Most policy is generated in central government, some in local government. Companies, charities and public and private organisations also have policies. For example, many banks and financial institutions have ethical and environmental codes that influence the way investments are made. In the United Kingdom, the Government has sought to encourage informed debate on matters of citizenship by improving access to the information on which policy is formulated. Digests of information are now published regularly, often linked to specific issues.

Management influences the way in which policy is translated into practice. Changes in national and regional economies resulting from new managerial strategies have an impact on ancillary industries by influencing the location of capital and enterprise, the demand for locally produced goods and services, opportunities for employment and the distribution of population. These changes influence the formal and informal systems of education and training through the demands they make for new knowledge, skills, processes, ways of obtaining, transforming and utilising information and participation in decision-making. Law, politics, economics and social concerns constrain all practical managerial decisions. Statutory duties may have to be reconciled with existing public rights. There are procedural rules for resolving conflict and organisational rules for the conduct of public power. Factors that are crucial for deciding what level and pattern of management can be afforded include the relationship between producers and consumers and how this is mediated through price mechanisms, supply and demand, the ways in which resources are distributed, and the roles of governmental and international organisations in regulating the economy and society. The increasing public accountability in policy-making required of governments, their agencies and public and private organisations has led to a demand for commensurate transparency in managerial practices. Documentation produced for the public is especially important educationally, as it is an effort to explain how policy is translated into practice and why particular managerial decisions are made.

The understanding of matters of citizenship that students have, the way they define themselves as citizens, and the values they hold are substantially influenced by popular information: newspapers, popular and semi-popular journals, magazines, television and the World Wide Web.

Journalism is inextricably linked with policy-making, management and interpretation, but differs from them in that it is not necessarily based on specialist knowledge. Expertise in communicating through the medium is generally preferred to specific qualifications. National newspapers have their specialist correspondents and may buy copy from specialist agencies, but the way in which the information is re-presented is ultimately at the discretion of the editor. Similarly, subject experts may be directly involved in the presentation of television programmes, but what the viewer sees is mediated through a director or producer. Journalism is highly selective in what it reports and how it reports it. Popular and semi-popular newspapers may present stories in a sensationalised way. Issues are often linked to high-profile or controversial personalities and geared towards conscience-salving, reassurance or scare-mongering. They often lack long-term vision and fail to signal complexity and interrelatedness. These characteristics are less evident in television documentaries. Complexity of issues is often signalled and longer-term perspectives are frequently presented although the content may still be highly selective. Bias and sensationalisation may be present in the television documentary, but usually it is far less blatant than in the popular press. There are dangers in extrapolating from particular issues to matters in general; however, research appears to support the observations of Lowe and Morrison (1984) that the nature of the arguments raised in documentaries is overtly moral rather than immediately political.

Such is the nature of the 'public information' that (i) informs students' views of policy and its enactment and interpretation, and (ii) interfaces with their formal studies in higher education. Most higher education is discipline-based. Discipline-based education breaks the link between experience and theory and encourages learners to believe that complex practical problems can be solved by using the resources of just one or two frameworks of thought. To extend this argument, the historical separation between formal education and the informal influences on students' experiences and understandings is also potentially limiting. There is a strong case for not only working across and between disciplines but also for developing integrating frameworks for dealing with information. Walker and Creanor (2005) identify four interrelated elements influencing learning events that cross boundaries:

1. the type of boundary;
2. the location of the boundary amongst the actors involved;
3. the role of the boundary;
4. the significance of the boundary.

All of these have to be taken into consideration in developing a pedagogy of connection for citizenship.

Not only are boundaries between formal knowledge structures and 'informal' sources of information inherent in policy-making and management but the processes of policy-making and management themselves establish boundaries by legitimising certain types of information. These boundaries are defended through processes of data-gathering and validation. Typically, the emphasis is on 'objective' knowledge of a situation. The associated values may be explicit or implicit.

The 'citizenship content' presented through news journalism is relatively unstable, that is, it is subject to transient judgements about topicality and newsworthiness. It is less likely to be concerned with verifiable claims, more with lines of argument. The processes involved in selecting and presenting information for a news item and its interpretation by the recipient are complex (Deacon et al. 1999). The more 'popular' the approach, the more value-laden the content. Popular journalism does not simply challenge beliefs and values; it may seek to overturn them.

The World Wide Web and its digital objects are altogether more complex. In addition to the considerations of representation and interpretation outlined above, digital objects and their associated networks suffer from a lack of centre, or controlling authority, and this raises questions about the source and nature of unity. Purves (1998) shows how writing and information technologies affect cultural and intellectual beliefs and structures, particularly in the context of organised religion. There are similar considerations about cross-disciplinary and cross-professional perspectives on citizenship, along with the attendant difficulties of working in what Purves (1998) describes as an anarchic (in the sense of being non-hierarchical and multidirectional) medium. The democratisation of information exchange, through sites like Wikipedia, and through social networking opens up new boundary issues.

A pedagogy of connection offers (i) a framework for conceptualising integrative work, in this case between formal knowledge structures and informal sources of information, and (ii) tools and interventions to facilitate integrative work. The framework focuses on the contexts of connection. A useful way of thinking of contexts is as niches that define the positions or roles of individuals within given situations, and states of competition between their beliefs, ideas and forms of behaviour (Dillon 2008a). Learning mediates transactions within these contexts or niches. Since learning is itself an activity, there is a sense in which the term 'active learning' is a tautology, especially when applied to citizenship, a notion that rests on a dynamic relationship encapsulated in the niche characterisation above.

The situation with which we are concerned arises as the boundaries between formal knowledge structures and informal sources of information that relate to citizenship. Students need to be aware of the different institutions and the actors involved in the situation and the transactions they broker across the boundaries. Situational analysis and transactional analysis may reveal the means by which gatekeepers maintain disciplinary and professional boundaries. The processes through which the actors and institutions select, validate and communicate information will depend on knowledge claims, which include disciplinary constructs and concepts, their justifications and verifications, the ways in which they are contested, the social and intellectual milieu in which they are developed and the use of discipline-specific or professionally located language and jargon (Dillon 2008b).

The moment they engage with these matters, students themselves become actors in the situation, and thus they need an understanding of their own values and positions relative to these boundaries.

There are many practical ways in which students can explore their beliefs and experiences. I have found that a set of questions based on the theories of reasoned action and planned behaviour (Ajzen 1988; Ajzen and Fishbein 1980) useful in getting students to explore their beliefs about environmental issues (Dillon and Gayford 1997). The theories of reasoned action and planned behaviour are concerned with the motivational forces that influence the way in which people intend to behave. There are three main influences on so-called 'behavioural intentions'. One is concerned with the beliefs that people have about the outcomes of their behaviour. Another is what people see as the social norms governing the particular behaviour, including what they think is likely to be approved of by their peers and how important peer approval is to them. The third is concerned with people's perceptions of how much personal control they have over a situation. Depending on the behaviour that is being studied, different parts of the model may be more or less influential.

The following are questions that students may ask about a situation, its boundaries, sources of information at the boundaries and where they stand relative to the situation, the information and the boundaries:

- What knowledge do I have of the situation and its boundaries?
- What are the sources of the information that have contributed to this knowledge?

- What are the compatibilities, contradictions and tensions in the information?
- Do I view the situation positively or negatively?
- What new information do I need to consolidate or challenge my view of the situation?
- What courses of action are open to influence the situation?
- What are the potential benefits of these actions?
- What are the potential disadvantages of these actions?
- How do I view the opinions of colleagues, friends and family about the situation and possible courses of action?
- What factors might influence my motivations to comply with these opinions?
- What control structures do I recognise in the situation?
- How do I see myself relative to these structures?
- Where do I now stand relative to the situation and its boundaries?
- What further information do I need?

Note that this list requires students to explore their knowledge and understanding, values, beliefs and emotions and to consider taking action. It is through action that citizenship is expressed.

In addition to revealing contexts, a pedagogy of connection utilises tools. Tools facilitate connections that enable students to engage in transitions that are of consequence, both in their thinking about a situation and in the actions they take within it, for example by adopting forms of behaviour which are compatible with espoused beliefs. Consequential transitions are where learners transform their understandings of themselves in relation to situations by connecting personal sense and other kinds of meaning (Beach 1999). To be of consequence, a transition in understanding or behaviour generally arises out of learning which has one or more of the following qualities:

- It is meaningful, that is, whatever is learnt is relevant to real needs and is connected to the prior knowledge of the individual concerned (e.g., Åhlberg 1998; Ausubel 1963; Novak and Gowin 1984).

- It is sceptical, that is, it implies questioning general regularities and 'received wisdom' (e.g., LeCompte 1994).
- It is deep, that is, it involves a search for evidence and justification for theory and practice and leads to metacognition – an understanding of the ways in which the individual thinks, learns and acts (e.g., Corno 1989; Greeno 1998; Jans and Leclercq 1997).
- It utilises both formal and informal situations, that is, it recognises the importance of planned and purposeful, objective-orientated learning and that individuals construct and continually adapt perceptual maps of the world and their place within it based on the totality of their experience (e.g., Åhlberg 1998; Nonaka and Takeuchi 1995; Polanyi 1966).
- It is receptive to the different ways of thinking, learning and working displayed by individuals, groups, teams and organisations in different situations and cultures (e.g., Fisher and Torbert 1995).
- It utilises both explicit knowledge and tacit knowledge. Explicit knowledge can be expressed accurately both verbally and in text as propositions and statements. Tacit knowledge is personal and is often difficult to express accurately in writing (e.g., Nonaka et al. 1996).
- It is cooperative and collaborative (e.g., Lieberman 1996).
- It is transferable, that is, the knowledge derived from it can be applied in new situations (e.g., Greeno 1998).
- It is creative, innovative, proactive, and future orientated (e.g., Mezirow 1996; Taylor 1997).

This is the list devised by Dillon and Åhlberg (2006) for characteristics of what they called 'high quality learning'. The greater the number of these characteristics involved in active learning, the greater the likelihood the educational transitions will be of consequence. To be of consequence, there has to be some conscious reflection, some struggling with ideas or issues, so as to invoke some hard questions about citizenship. When 'internalised', the outcomes of the transitions become part of the individual's repertoire of psychological tools (Kozulin 1998). In other words, he or she has the intellectual means to express convictions and justify beliefs and actions.

Tools that support consequential transitions typically involve making connections, for example, comparison, association, analogy, metaphor, mapping and blending. These tools facilitate the movement of concepts and constructs in boundary transactions between disciplines. In addition, tools that enable information to be evaluated and arguments constructed or refuted are important in active learning for citizenship. Analysis of reasoning, rhetoric and argumentation (ARRA) is such a tool. It is a scheme for analysing an argument by finding the theoretical and empirical grounds for it, the claims made, the justifications for the claims and potential refutations of the claims. It may also be used for constructing a rational and well-reasoned argument by setting out the theoretical and empirical grounds for it, constructing claims, finding rationale justifications for them and anticipating potential refutations. ARRA is good for dealing with complex problems, especially where different people make contradictory claims.

Toulmin (1958) is a seminal work on argumentation discourse. Åhlberg (1998) adapted and extended Toulmin's argumentation analysis, eventually arriving at the ARRA scheme presented in the appendix. ARRA is broadly compatible with Scriven's (1976) list of the steps necessary to analyse everyday arguments and reasoning:

- Clarification of the meaning of what is said or written, what is reasoned or argued.
- Identification of the conclusions or claims (stated or unstated).
- Portrayal of the structure of reasoning.

- Formulation of the stated and unstated assumptions (missing premises).
- Criticism of both premises (given and missing) and inferences (given and missing).
- Overall evaluation of the reasoning and argumentation.

The example of ARRA given in the appendix is based on a short, contrived, journalistic text about environmentalist Mark Lynas's critique in *The Ecologist* of Bjørn Lomborg's book *The Skeptical Environmentalist,* in which Lomborg casts doubt on claims for an environmental crisis. The argument is set in the context of education for sustainable development. It is a classic example of the power of information and claims about misinformation in both sides of an argument in which there is considerable public interest. Through the ARRA, statements and arguments are analysed systematically. The structure of the argument and its robustness emerge. The ARRA reveals the loci of the argument, the points at which there is the greatest backing, qualification or refutation of the argument. ARRA is a laboured process but worth undertaking occasionally as it foregrounds the essential elements and processes in the chain of reasoning and argumentation. With practice, and when the tool has been internalised (Kozulin 1998), it is possible to make a preliminary appraisal of a text or an argument without undertaking a formal ARRA.

The emphasis in ARRA is on analysis and rationality, but a pedagogy of connection should also invite students to identify tensions and make connections with their personal experiences and prior learning. Taking all of its elements together, the pedagogy of connection should develop a combination of analytical, integrative and synthetic forms of thinking and being (Sternberg and Lubart 1999). Understanding how ideas and concepts are developed within the formal knowledge structures of disciplines, and how these structures may be challenged by informal sources of information involves analytical thinking. Moving ideas between knowledge structures and combining information from new sources involves integrative thinking. Recognising new patterns that emerge from reconfigurations of beliefs, ideas and concepts and developing new frameworks to accommodate them involves synthetic thinking. Translating these forms of thinking into actions that are compatible with beliefs and that can be performed with integrity is citizenship made real.

Acknowledgement

I am grateful to Professor Mauri Åhlberg, University of Helsinki, for the example of analysis of reasoning, rhetoric and argumentation.

References

Åhlberg, M. (1998) 'Education for Sustainability, Good Environment and Good Life', in M. Åhlberg and W. Leal Filho (eds), *Environmental Education for Sustainability: Good Environment, Good Life,* Frankfurt am Main, Peter Lang, pp. 25–43.

Ajzen, I. (1988) *Attitudes, Personality and Behaviour,* Milton Keynes: Open University Press.

Ajzen, I. and Fishbein, M. (1980) *Understanding Attitudes and Predicting Social Behaviour,* Englewood Cliffs, NJ: Prentice-Hall.

Ausubel, D. (1963) *The Psychology of Meaningful Verbal Learning,* New York: Grune and Stratton.

Beach, K. (1999) 'Consequential Transitions: A Sociocultural Expedition Beyond Transfer in Education', *Review of Research in Education,* 24: 101–39.

Beck, J. (1996) 'Citizenship Education: Problems and Possibilities', *Curriculum Studies,* 4: 349–66.

Corno, L. (1989) 'Self-Regulated Learning: a Volitional Analysis', in B. Zimmerman and D. Schunk (eds), *Self-Regulated Learning and Academic Achievement: Theory, Research and Practice,* New York: Springer.

Deacon, D., Fenton, N. and Bryman, A. (1999) 'From Inception to Reception: The Natural History of a News Item', *Media, Culture and Society,* 21: 5–31.

Dillon, P. J. (2006) 'Creativity, Integrativism and a Pedagogy of Connection', *International Journal of Thinking Skills and Creativity,* 1 (2): 69–83.

Dillon, P. J. (2008a) 'Creativity, Wisdom and Trusteeship: Niches of Cultural Production', in A. Craft, H. Gardner and G. Claxton (eds), *Creativity and Wisdom in Education,* Thousand Oaks, Calif.: Corwin Press, pp. 105–18.

Dillon, P. J. (2008b) 'A Pedagogy of Connection and Boundary Crossings: Methodological and Epistemological Transactions in Working Across and Between Disciplines', *Innovations in Education and Teaching International,* 45 (3): 255–62.

Dillon, P. J. and Gayford, C. G. (1997) 'A Psychometric Approach to Investigating the Environmental Beliefs, Intentions and Behaviours of Pre-Service Teachers', *Environmental Education Research,* 3 (3): 283–98.

Dillon, P. J. and Åhlberg, M. (2006) 'Integrativism as a Theoretical and Organisational Framework for E-Learning and Practitioner Research', *Technology, Pedagogy and Education,* 15 (1): 7–30.

Fisher, D. and Torbert, W. (1995) *Personal and Organizational Transformations,* London: McGraw-Hill.

Greeno, J., (1998) 'The Situativity of Knowing, Learning and Research', *American Psychologist,* 53 (1): 5–26.

Jans, V. and Leclercq, D. (1997) 'Metacognitive Realism: A Cognitive Style or a Learning Strategy', *Educational Psychology,* 17 (1–2): 101–10.

Kozulin, A. (1998) *Psychological Tools: A Sociocultural Approach to Education,* Cambridge, Mass.: Harvard University Press.

LeCompte, M. D. (1994) 'Defining Reality: Applying Double Description and Chaos Theory to the Practice of Practice', *Educational Theory,* 44 (3): 277–98.

Lieberman, A. (1996) 'Creating Intentional Learning Communities', *Educational Leadership,* 54 (3): 51–5.

Lomborg, B. (2001) *The Skeptical Environmentalist: Measuring the Real State of the World,* Cambridge: Cambridge University Press.

Lowe, and Morrison, D. (1984) 'Bad News or Good News: Politics and the Mass Media', *The Sociological Review,* 31 (1): 75–90.

Lynas, M. (2003) 'Natural Bjorn Killer', *The Ecologist,* 33 (2): 26–9.

Marshall, T. H. (1950) *Citizenship and Social Class and Other Essays,* Cambridge: Cambridge University Press.

Mezirow, J. (1996) 'Contemporary Paradigms of Learning', *Adult Education Quarterly,* 46 (3): 158–73.

Nonaka, I. and Takeuchi, H. (1995) *The Knowledge-Creating Company,* New York: Oxford University Press.

Nonaka, I., Takeuchi, H. and Umemuto, K. (1996) 'A Theory of Organisational Knowledge Creation', *International Journal of Technology Management,* 11 (7/8): 833–45.

Novak, J. and Gowin, B. (1984) *Learning How to Learn,* Cambridge: Cambridge University Press.

Polanyi, M. (1966) *Tacit Knowledge,* London: Routledge & Kegan Paul.

Purves, A. C. (1998) *The Web of Text and the Web of God,* New York: Guilford.

Scriven, M. (1976) *Reasoning,* New York: McGraw-Hill.

Star, S. L. and Griesemer, J. R. (1989) 'Institutional Ecology, "Translations" and Boundary Objects: Amateurs and Professionals in Berkeley's Museum of Vertebrate Zoology, 1907–39', *Social Studies in Science,* 19: 387–420.

Sternberg, R. J. and Lubart, T. I. (1999) 'The Concept of Creativity: Prospects and Paradigms', in R. J. Sternberg (ed.), *Handbook of Creativity,* Cambridge: Cambridge University Press, pp. 3–15.

Taylor, E. (1997) 'Building Upon the Theoretical Debate: A Critical Review of the Empirical Studies of Mezirow's Transformative Learning Theory', *Adult Education Quarterly,* 48: 34–59.

Toulmin, S. (1958) *Uses of Argument,* Cambridge: Cambridge University Press.

Walker, S. and Creanor, L. (2005) 'Crossing Complex Boundaries: Transnational Online Education in European Trade Unions', *Journal of Computer Assisted Learning,* 21: 343–54.

Appendix: Analysis of Reasoning, Rhetoric and Argumentation

The basic categories of ARRA are as follows:

Code	Description of the code
C	Claim or conclusion about a situation.
G	Ground or evidence for the claim.
W	Warrant – justifies either the claim or a connection between a ground and a claim by appealing to concrete, observable evidence. It may be a document, diagram, article, picture, model, analogy, etc.
B	Backing – abstract justification for the claim, ground or warrant. It may be a theory, value, common practice, etc.
Q	Qualification – qualifies a claim by expressing degrees of confidence, probability or likelihood e.g. 'always', 'often', 'perhaps', etc.
R	Refutation – states the conditions under which a claim does not hold or the limits within which the claim is valid.
q	Real question – for which an answer is expected.
rq	Rhetorical question – for which no answer is expected.
e	Emotional expression.

Table 5.1

Statements and arguments are analysed systematically by assigning the codes listed above to various parts of the text. The structure of the argument and its robustness emerge. An example is given in the table below. It is an analysis, in the context of education for sustainable development, of a short, contrived, journalistic text about an environmental argument reported in *The Ecologist*.

The text is as follows:

> Has the quality of the global environment
> continually got worse or has it improved during

the last decades? According to Bjorn Lomborg (2001) it has improved. According to an article in the journal *The Ecologist,* written by Mark Lynas (2003) it has become worse. The title of Lynas's article is 'Natural Bjorn Killer'. The writer attacks Bjorn Lomborg both in print and personally (he splashed a cream cake into Lomborg's face – a photograph is shown of how Lomborg looked after the incidence. The differences in their claims (opinions) are questions that can be answered empirically using ARRA. It is evident that modern societies are in many ways unsustainable (Lomborg 2001, Lynas 2003). If we want sustainable societies, a better environment and a high quality of life, then we ought to promote learning, thinking and acting for sustainable development. Unless we think that things are not so bad after all, in which case why bother? Or unless we think that there is no hope of survival for humankind. Again, why bother? A critical scientific realist admits that there is plenty to do for continual improvement of all human processes to promote sustainable development, including education for sustainable development.

Analysis of the text may be tabulated and the chain of reasoning shown:

Text	Codes
Has the quality of the global environment continually got worse or has it improved during the last decades?	q1
According to Bjorn Lomborg (2001) it has improved.	C1, W1
According to an article in the journal *The Ecologist*, written by Mark Lynas (2003) it has become worse.	C2, W2
The title of Lynas's article is 'Natural Bjorn killer'.	C3, e1
The writer attacks Bjorn Lomborg both in print and personally (he splashed a cream cake into Lomborg's face - a photograph is shown of how Lomborg looked after the incidence).	C4
The differences in their claims (opinions) are questions that can be answered empirically using ARRA.	e2
It is evident that modern knowledge societies are in many ways unsustainable (Lomborg 2001, Lynas 2003).	C5, C6
If we want sustainable societies, a better environment and a high quality of life, then we ought to promote learning, thinking and acting for sustainable development.	C7
Unless we think that things are not so bad after all, In which case why bother?	W1, W2
Or unless we think that there is no hope of survival of humankind.	
Again, why bother?	
A critical scientific realist admits that there are plenty to do for continual improvement of all human processes to promote sustainable development, including education for sustainable development.	

Table 5.2

The chain of reasoning and argumentation can be represented as:

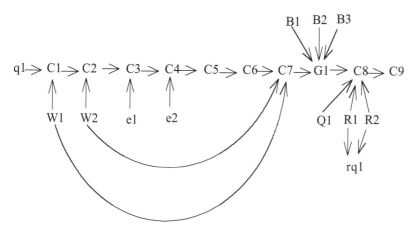

Figure 5.1

Part II: Active Citizenship

Chapter 6

Social and Moral Responsibility

Janet Kay

Social and moral responsibility is one of the three themes of citizenship education outlined in the Crick Report (1998). The Crick Report states that the development of social and moral responsibility is a prerequisite of citizenship, in respect of a required understanding of the consequences of one's actions and the impact of these actions on others. Underpinning this theme is the sense that there needs to be a much clearer focus on developing social and moral responsibility, in terms of respect for the rights of others and the relationship between the individual and the community, in young people. As such, Crick argued that citizenship education requires young people to learn about moral values and to develop their ability to apply these in practice (1998). However, on publication of the report, it was suggested that this theme was possibly the most controversial of the three, because while a moral dimension to citizenship education avoids the 'dry' civic approach, it also begs the question as to which moral values, in a pluralist society, young people should be learning (Pyke 2002).

Moral responsibility implies a knowledge and understanding of 'right' and 'wrong' and the ability and willingness to behave morally. As such, citizenship education in this area focuses on developing individuals' ability to act as moral agents in their choices, intentions and actions. Social responsibility suggests that an individual has responsibility to the community or society in terms of choices about behaviour. One aspect of this is legal responsibility, i.e. the responsibility of a citizen to act within the law. However, the concept of social responsibility implies a more active role than remaining law-abiding, encompassing the notion that individuals should support and protect their societies' interests and that they should be more broadly accountable to their communities for their actions.

Higher Education and Social and Moral Development

In Higher Education Institutions, the development of social and moral responsibility through the transmission of values has been seen as problematical since the certainties of religious doctrine have diminished since the nineteenth century. Sandolow (1991) argues that modern concepts of morality are based on the view that morality is a social construct, suggesting that the current debate focuses not so much on absolutes about what is moral or not but on how we deal with questions about what has been constructed.

With little consensus about what is morality, educationalists are left with the unenviable task of supporting the development of social and moral responsibility without a certain framework on which to base this process. However, some believe that the role of HEIs in this process has become central because of that very uncertainty. Sandolow (1991) argues that as both large influential conglomerates and as centres of education, HEIs have a role in supporting moral development. Sandolow adopts Feinberg's (1968) view that collective social responsibility is the concern of large institutions and that while their primary purpose may not be to pursue social justice, it is still part of their role. In addition, the view that HEIs should be concerned with moral issues persists, implying that students need to be viewed as members of a community and not just as customers.

Wilcox and Ebbs (1992) echo this view, stating that, as HEIs are a source of knowledge they are also powerful and capable of influencing social and economic life. Harkavy (2006), however, suggests that often the rhetoric of HEIs does not match outcomes. While HEIs may support the promotion of citizenship values and practices, the commercialisation of higher education 'powerfully legitimises and reinforces the pursuit of economic self-interest by students' (Harkavy 2006: 14). This begs the question as to whether higher education has moved in purpose from the ethical, social and character development that was evident in the past, to a focus on discipline-led training for specific employment purposes (Holland 1991). This implies that students may have 'utilitarian' motives for entering higher education, focusing on achieving qualifications for a career, rather than a broader educational experience (Jones and Thomas 2005). This is confirmed by Kuh (2005) cited in Hersch and Schneider (2005), who reported that in the previous decade there was a significant decrease in the number of students who had reported developments in their values and ethics during their time in higher education. In addition, Cleaver et al. (2005) found that schools encountered significant difficulties in involving pupils in decision-making, which resonates with the experience of HEIs.

In consumer-driven market economies, in which the distribution of wealth, power and status dominate, it is difficult to see where the notion of individual moral responsibility may lie. Sandolow (1991) argues this point and suggests that HEIs are critiqued from both conservative and liberal standpoints for teaching neither the ethics of individual moral responsibility nor a commitment to improving society through social change. Carr (1999) proposes that there are two questions involved: the 'proper direction' of moral education and whether what happens in our educational institutions can improve public behaviour. The problem is when moral education focuses only on issues of social order and the inculcation of desirable social habits. Although this is generally seen as part of the moral educational process, it is problematical to consider an education that goes beyond this and tackling issues of 'absolute and universal moral significance' (Carr 1999: 26). Carr warns us to be careful not to confuse 'moral education and social engineering', because although the latter may be positively affected by success in the former, they are not the same thing.

Hersch and Schneider (2005) argue that despite the difficulties, this is not an issue HEIs can duck. Moral messages are part of what takes place in HEIs and, as they cannot be ignored, these messages must not be left to chance (Colby et al. 2003). Hersch and Schneider (2005) suggest that concerns about imposing moral values on students and the fragmentation of ethical certainties may suggest that others' social and moral responsibility is 'none of our business'. However, the authors discount this view on the basis that whether formally planned or not, being part of a higher-education community will convey moral values and influence the development of students' social and moral responsibility. If this is the case, then HEIs need to consider the ways in which that influence is best expressed.

Wilcox and Ebbs (1992) promote the view that it is important to analyse the ethics of the ethos of the whole institution, in terms of culture, customs and practices across the institutional structures. The key issue is the impact of this ethos on the quality of life. As such, 'Responsibility for individual and social welfare is part of the institutional landscape, a daily occurrence manifested in decision making on all levels of the college or university and in the goals toward which the decision making is directed' (Wilcox and Ebbs 1992: 1). The quality of the ethical environment is significant to students' overall experience of higher education and the ways in which they negotiate ethical issues and their own experiences.

The Concept of Morality

There is no doubt that the concept of morality is disputed, but Wilson (1990) reminds us that there is a difference between words and concepts. While 'moral' may mean different things in different contexts, the concept of morality is common. Hersch et al. (1980) state that morality has three elements: caring (involving social motivation and social knowledge); judging (making judgements about competing moral issues in relation to a consistent moral principle); and acting (an action not being moral or immoral in itself but dependent on the caring and judging it is based on).

However, defining morality is complex, and Wilson (1990: 82) draws on Plato and Aristotle's deliberations to suggest that 'the central use of "moral" refers to a certain set of underlying dispositions, to the basic ecology . . . of human desires, emotions and deeds'. Wilson goes on to argue that morality is not something we can accept or reject as suggested by Warnock (1971) because it underpins all human activities, even those concerned with non-moral issues. Eshelman (2004) states than any theory of moral responsibility should discuss the concept of moral responsibility; the criteria for being a moral agent; the conditions under which moral responsibility is properly applied (where an agent has acted with free will and is able to make choices) and 'objects of responsibility ascriptions' (those things that we can ascribe moral responsibility to such as actions or non-actions).

A key part of this discussion is how morality can be determined. Concerns about determining the moral virtues have given way to focusing on trying to determine what is moral behaviour and what is not and criteria or principles for determining what is right and what is wrong. These questions have a different significance since the hegemony of the church in determining absolute moral values gave way to more individualistic and subjective views of values during the Reformation (Carr 1999). Subsequent theories of morality focus more on the role of moral reasoning in achieving human goals rather than any absolute concept of moral values.

As such, normative ethical theories emerged, dealing with efforts to determine how right and wrong can be classified and translated into rules for human conduct. Consequentialist theories hold that it is the consequences of an action that determine its morality, not the character of the action itself. So the morality of an action is determined retrospectively, based on the outcomes of the action, and a morally positive action is one that produces good consequences (Eshelmen 2004). Deontological theories focus on the morality of an action as inherent in the act itself and not in the outcomes of that act. As such, consequentialism implies that humans do not have to have moral intentions to produce moral outcomes, whereas deontological theorists assume that morally good intentions are morality, whatever the outcomes.

The issue that arises from both these theoretical bases is the implication that a value judgement about what is 'right' and what is 'wrong' or what is a 'good' outcome or a 'bad' outcome has to be made. This begs the question as to whether all assumptions of morality are subjective and relative. Ayer (1948) (cited in McPhail 1982) argues that there is no 'truth value' to moral statements as they merely reflect the individuals' moral beliefs and are entirely subjective. He suggested that moral discussion focuses on the advisability of accepting or rejecting an action or viewpoint but 'discredits the logical authority of moral statements because the criteria for logical verification cannot be established' (McPhail 1982: 21). If we, then, reject the existence of universal moral laws, then are all moral standpoints individually or socially determined within specific cultural contexts? If this is the case, then the promotion of morality through education could be viewed as part of the socialisation of an individual into a group (community) by inculcating a particular culturally determined view or perspective of what morality is. Is morality therefore nothing more than a collection of cultural norms to be passed on to new citizens-in-the-making? And, as such, is moral education merely a process by which these cultural norms are passed on to citizens-to-be to ensure their social compliance? McPhail (1982) argues that morality can stand beyond the social norms and therefore include both inculcation into these norms and evaluation and criticism of these. However, this discussion brings us back to the basic question of why we should be moral in terms of concern for others and their needs, and whether incentives to morality are intrinsic or relate to personal gratification or gain.

Morality and the Individual

Determining what is moral is one significant aspect of the debate, but another rests on the notion of whether individuals can be moral. The concept of moral responsibility rests on the idea that individuals can be held responsible for their actions and therefore be judged as to the morality of these. This presupposes that individuals are free to make choices about their actions. One of the problematical issues in discussing moral responsibility is the extent to which this is the case. Can we really be held morally responsible for our actions? The notion of being responsible or being held responsible implies that the individual can make choices and decisions unencumbered and without duress – in fact, by exercising free will.

The extent to which free will actually exists has occupied philosophers from ancient Greece onwards. The concept of free will was acknowledged in early Greek texts in terms of ascribing praise or blame to actions and acknowledging that some actions were free of praise or blame (excused) because they were coerced, as the agent's freedom to choose had been compromised (Eshelman 2004). Aristotle theorised that moral responsibility can be judged in individuals who are moral agents and who are able to act voluntarily. Moral agents are those who have the capacity to make deliberate decisions about their actions, based on their concept of what is 'good'. Voluntary action implies that the agent chooses to act and is aware of their actions. Eshelman (2004) suggests an ambiguity in Aristotle's theory, based on the appropriateness of judging others behaviour as moral. He argues that this ambiguity centres round whether Aristotle's view of moral responsibility is merit-based (praise or blame given because the agent deserves this) or consequentialist (praise or blame given because it may bring about improvements in the agent's behaviour or character). However, the key theme is the extent to which free will exists and whether the presence or absence of free will determines the ability to act morally.

Hard determinists argue that free will is impossible in a world where events and actions are causally determined by a chain of prior occurrences, bringing into question the ability of individuals to make rational and free choices about their actions. Without free will, the individual cannot be held morally responsible for actions which are predetermined and outside that individual's control. The debate about whether the concepts of free will and determinism can be held simultaneously has dominated discussion about whether humans can be held responsible for their actions. Compatibilists argue that these two apparently opposing concepts can be reconciled as behaviour needs to be determined, rather than random, for the actor to be held responsible for it. Free will is dependent on choices being deliberately and consciously made and the existence of choice, in that the actor could have acted otherwise than they did. The question then arises as to whether free will does exist. Can individuals really make choices and act freely?

According to Honderich (1988), the compatibilism/incompatibilism argument is not the only way of assessing the impact of determinism on the concept of free will. He suggests that moral responsibility depends on our attitudes to others' actions, which involve aesthetic attitudes relating to our withdrawal from repugnant behaviour and retributive attitudes, which relate to our desire to disapprove, blame or punish this behaviour. However, we cannot sustain retributive attitudes if we do not believe others are responsible for their behaviours. As such, Honderich suggest two models of moral responsibility. If we are able to make choices and are responsible for these (voluntariness and origination) then we have free will but this is incompatible with determinism. If we are only able to make choices but cannot be responsible for these (voluntariness only) then we have free will that is compatible with determinism.

Honderich (1988) argues the significance of consequentialism, suggesting through his 'principle of humanity' that morality is associated with behaviour that helps others out of 'bad' lives. Morality is therefore linked to our actions or omissions in terms of this process as we have moral responsibility for 'bad' lives. Decision-making on whether an action is moral or not should be based on the consequences of that action only (Anscombe 1958). This begs the question of how the morality of specific actions can be judged in terms of consequences as these may be different for different individuals, groups or communities affected by such actions. Raillon (1984) argues that there can be tension between the individuals' interests and the interests of the community in determining the morality of an action, where the outcomes differ for each. He suggests that individuals will be more concerned with the outcomes for themselves and those close to them than they will for the wider community. Downie (1964) also suggested that the extent of moral responsibility may be determined according to the social roles that individuals adopt within their social context. Social roles may impact on the individual's freedom to act from choice. For example, an individual may choose not to kill another human as part of his or her freely chosen moral behaviour but may kill others in the social role of a combatant in war.

Moral Responsibility

Strawson (1974) suggests that social contexts are important for our understanding of moral responsibility, in terms of the significance of interpersonal relationships to the extent to which we hold others morally responsible. Strawson argued that we cannot hold others to be morally responsible because of their being morally responsible. Our attitudes to holding others morally responsible are not value-free but are dependent on our subjective views of what that person's behaviour means in terms of their attitudes to us – our reactions to whether this behaviour indicated good will or otherwise towards us. Strawson described this response as a participant-reactive attitude. However, this attitude can be suspended and a more objective stance taken if we do not believe that the other is fully part of the social and moral community (such as young children or mentally ill people). Strawson argues that judgements about moral responsibility are dependent on the reactive attitude to the other's behaviour, rather than on our belief that the other is morally responsible. However, Wilson (1990) suggests that Strawson makes too much of the link between morality and action, although the distinction between individual and social moral needs is relevant.

Eshelman (2004) suggests that the most recent views on morality focus on responsibility as attributability and responsibility as accountability. Attributability is related to the notion of self and accountability to the concept of moral responsibility in a social context so that behaviour is governed by the expectations we have of each other. Within this concept, holding someone responsible is essentially a social act, based on belonging to a shared moral community. Moral responsibility can be seen in this context as the extent to which individuals support or undermine the well-being of the community, suggesting that morality is indeed a culturally determined set of norms and that conformity to these is moral behaviour. This view is contested on the basis that we must not equate social conformity with morality, because one of the key aspects of developing morality is the development of moral reasoning.

These debates reflect the uncertainties about how moral and social responsibility can be conceptualised and promoted within modern societies. Adrift from moral certainties and wary of merely promoting dominant cultural norms, the role of moral reasoning and the ability to rationally choose between moral values is at the forefront, but it still leaves us with a concern that such choices may lack a coherent value-base or 'morality'. The debate leads us to question how we promote moral and social responsibility in young people as part of their learning in higher education in ways that not only promote moral reasoning but also develop values and ethical stances that go beyond, and can contest, the social norms of the times.

Educating for Social and Moral Responsibility

Key questions in terms of developing social and moral responsibility in educational settings remain problematical. Is there a difference between moral education and social engineering to improve public behaviour? How can we resolve issues about the fluid and contextual notion of moral values? And are we truly able to be held morally responsible for our actions in a deterministic world? Hersch et al. (1980: 14) suggest that the purpose of moral education in the nineteenth century was to promote a 'narrow form of socialization'. However, in the twentieth century, this narrowness was challenged by philosophers such as Dewey (1909, 1938) who argued that morality was a dynamic not static concept, linked to the changing values of modern democracies. Dewey believed that moral education needed to be rooted in the development of reasoning, not in training children to be dutiful to fixed moral rules. As such, Dewey's arguments suggest that moral education and education per se are the same thing as they both involve the use of reason to resolve issues.

However, liberal educationalists such as Dewey were challenged in their belief that learning the ability to reflect on values rationally was sufficient to develop moral responsibility. According to Carr (1999), liberal educationalists in a secular world sought to promote 'rational moral autonomy' to prepare individuals for their role in an individualistic market economy and to maximise the chances of positive life choices. This notion of morality is rooted in concepts of individual rights and reciprocal relationships between individuals rather than the absolute moral values of previous times. Jonathan (1999) suggests that liberal moral education supports the development of individuals as moral agents who are equipped to reflect on the range of values they encounter and make considered moral judgements about these. Kohlberg (1981) supports this approach through his theory of moral development. Theorising that moral development is achieved through stages in progress towards increasingly sophisticated moral reasoning signifies that such moral reasoning is the 'central feature of morality and moral education' (Straughan 1982: 19).

Wilson (1990) argues that moral relativism does not make all values and beliefs arbitrary. He suggests that the answer to problems of relativity in moral thinking should be answered by closer focus on the processes of thinking about and rationalising moral issues. However, Carr (1999: 38) concludes that liberal moral education, with its tolerance of a wide range of moral perspectives, excluding those which infringed on individual rights, failed to establish or explore 'which human goals are worthier of pursuit than others'. Straughan (1982) suggests that the determining the content of moral education is problematical because nothing can be categorically determined as morally right and that moral agents need to be able to make rational judgements and choices to be moral. However, he also argues that whereas following the dictates of an external moral authority has no value as a basis for moral development, developing a rational conscience, in which the moral authority is internalised, has.

Jonathan (1999) also states that the development of critical reasoning is not sufficient in moral education as it does not in itself provide the framework upon which to develop and structure moral values. However, responses to the perceived crisis of moral decline vary. Straughan (1982) suggested that the perception that a moral vacuum had entered the classroom, as the declining influence of religion severed society from moral certainties, was a flawed concept. Straughan argues that the 'moralistic argument' 'is untenable as it is not possible to educate for moral certainties or to teach children "to be good"' (1982: 9). Straughan suggests that while educators affect value neutrality and value clarification to support the development of individual moral reasoning, in fact values are transmitted through in all educational institutions through pedagogical choices and practices.

Wilcox and Ebbs (1992) suggest that the learning community is the key element in supporting the 'scholar teacher/researcher' to balance individual and group needs. The learning community provides coherence to the experience of members and supports the development of an ethical basis for the institution as a whole. In this context, learning communities in higher education are conceptualised as being ideally based on collectivist cultures, which oppose the individualisation of learning and academic interests common to institutions in recent times.

It is clear that the role of HEIs must go beyond simply supporting the development of rational thinking in students in value-free ways. The culture and ethos of the institution needs to promote the development of social and moral responsibility in more active and committed ways, which support the student to negotiate the competing demands of self and others.

Ethos and Active Learning

Dewey (1909, 1938) strongly advocated active-learning approaches to moral education, arguing that participation and reflection were the keys to learning moral values. In this way, learning about morality becomes practising moral behaviour in a variety of social situations. This view has implications for education in social and moral responsibility today, as according to Dewey, this simply cannot be achieved through classroom teaching but must be achieved through collective participation in meaningful activities and institutions, which promote learning through experience, enquiry and reflection.

'Even if the teacher introduced concepts such as democracy, justice, respect for others and human rights, if the classroom and school structure continued to model and enforce authoritarian social relations, no effective learning would take place' (Hersch et al. 1980: 21).

McPhail (1982) suggests that Dewey's ideas are relevant to pluralist societies in which moral values and bases may be contested and the rights of the individual and groups may at time conflict. Sandolow (1991) also suggests supporting student 'character development' through active learning that develops both student knowledge and their ability to think rationally, as a way forward from the apparent impasse in HEIs around moral development.

Farbo (2006) also supports the introduction of engagement pedagogies but warned that they must not be merely seen as instructional innovation. HEIs must create the conditions for learning about moral and social issues through their structures and functions in order for this to be a meaningful experience. In his review of Dewey's work, Smith (2001) suggests that educational institutions need to reflect the ideals that they are supporting in their own structures and functions, by democratising relationships between students and teachers. Smith also cites Winch and Gingell (1999) who argue that schools need to reconsider the authoritarian nature of the type of relationships they promote if they want their pupils to learn democratic values. It is difficult to see how this does not also apply to

HEIs. Democratic relationships are only one aspect of effective learning communities for citizenship; Hersch and Schneider (2005) suggest that there needs to be a significant and 'pervasive' cultural change to ensure that HEIs can educate for moral responsibility.

Nixon suggests that the way forward is a 'new Aristotelianism' (2004: 115) informed by both the Socratic idea of negative wisdom and the moral imperative to take the 'right action'. Negative wisdom involves the questioning of false assumptions and therefore involvement in rational debate, whereas the 'right action' implies involvement in social and community issues and living a 'good' life. Combining these two notions suggest that a 'good' life can be lived despite the lack of moral certainties. Within this notion, learning is associated with agency and social engagement. Students need to practise social and moral responsibility through engaging with others in learning about their world, rather than learning about citizenship issues in theory. Pedagogies that promote rational debate and reflection need to be promoted in the context of exploring social and moral issues in 'real-life' contexts. In this way, learning becomes the medium for social engagement and participation.

Conclusion

The effectiveness of HEIs in supporting the development of students' social and moral responsibility rests on an holistic approach, encompassing the institutional ethos, culture, structures and pedagogies. While active learning focusing on engagement and rational debate can support the development of students' ability to recognise and consider ethical issues, the environment in which this takes place must reflect an ethos that promotes positive relationships and values such as respect, honesty and caring.

Mass-market, consumerist approaches to higher education may fail to provide students with the necessary environment in which social and moral development can take place effectively. Students need opportunities to engage in learning communities that both respect their individuality and support their involvement with others in mutually created learning experiences that nurture debate and challenge their thinking.

References

Anscombe, G. E. M. (1958) 'Modern Moral Philosophy', *Philosophy*, 33: 38–40.

Carr, D. (1999) 'Cross Questions and Crooked Answers: Contemporary Problems for Moral Education', in J. Mark Halstead and T. H. McLaughlin (eds), *Education in Morality*, London: Routledge.

Cleaver, E., Ireland, E., Kerr, D. and Lopes, J. (2005) *Citizenship Education Longitudinal Study: Second Cross-Sectional Survey 2004. Listening to Young People: Citizenship Education in England (DfES Research Report 626)*, London: DfES.

Colby, A., Ehrlich, T., Beaumont, E., and Stephens, J. (2003) 'Pedagogical Strategies for Educating Citizens', in A. Colby et al. (eds), *Educating Citizens: Preparing America's Undergraduates for Lives of Moral and Civic Responsibility*, San Francisco, Calif.: Jossey-Bass.

Citizenship Advisory Group (1998) *Education for Citizenship and the Teaching of Democracy in Schools: Final Report of the Advisory Group on Citizenship (the 'Crick' Report')*, London: Qualifications and Curriculum Authority.

Dewey, J. (1909) *Moral Principles in Education*, Boston, Mass.: Houghton Mifflin Company.

—— (1938) *Experience and Education*, New York: Collier Books.

Downie, R. S. (1964) 'Social Roles and Moral Responsibility', *Philosophy*, 39 (147): 29–36.

Eshelman, A. (2004) 'Moral Responsibility', *Stanford Encyclopedia of Philosophy*, available online at http://www.seop.leeds.ac.uk/entries/moral-responsibility.

Farbo, M. (2006) 'Dare American Higher Education Build a New Social Order? In the Service of Whom and the Promotion of What in the Education', in B. Holland and J. Meeropol (eds), *A More Perfect Vision: The Future of Campus Engagement*, Providence, RI: Campus Compact. Available online at http://www.compact.org/20th/papers.

Feinberg, J. (1968) 'Collective Responsibility', *Journal of Philosophy*, 65 (21): 222–51.

Harkavy, I. (2006) 'The Role of Universities in Advancing Citizenship and Social Justice in the 21st Century', *Education, Citizenship and Social Justice*, 1 (1): 5–37.

Hersch, R. H., Miller, J. P. and Fielding, G. D. (1980) *Models of Moral Education*, New York: Longman Inc.

Hersh, R. H. and Schneider, C. G. (2005) 'Fostering Personal and Social Responsibility on College and University Campuses', *Liberal Education*.

Holland, J. R. (1991) 'Moral Values in Higher Education', in D. L. Thomson (ed.), *Moral Values and Higher Education*, New York: Suny Press.

Honderich, T. (1988) *The Consequences of Determinism: A Theory of Determinism*, Vol. II, London: Clarendon.

Jonathan, R. (1999) 'Agency and Contingency in Moral Development and Education', in J. Mark Halstead and T. H. McLaughlin (eds), *Education in Morality*, London: Routledge.

Jones, R. and Thomas, L. (2005) 'The 2003 UK Government Higher Education White Paper: a Critical Assessment of Its Implications for the Success of the Widening Participation Agenda', *Journal of Education Policy,* 20 (5): 615–630.

Kohlberg, L. (1981) *The Philosophy of Moral Development: Moral Stages and the Idea of Justice,* New York: Harper & Row.

Kuh, G. (2005) 'Do Environments Matter? A Comparative Analysis of the Impress of Different Types of Colleges and Universities on Character', *Journal of College and Character,* available online at http://www.collegevalues.org/articles.cfm?a=1&id=239.

McPhail (1982) *Social and Moral Education,* Oxford: Blackwell.

Nixon, J. (2004) 'Learning the Language of Deliberative Democracy', in M. Walker and J. Nixon (eds), *Reclaiming Universities from a Runaway World,* Buckingham: Open University Press.

Pyke, N. (2002) 'Citizenship: Critical Thinking Not Propaganda', *Independent,* 27 September.

Raillon (1984) 'Alienation, Consequentialism and the Demands of Morality', *Philosophy and Public Affairs,* 13 (2): 134–71.

Sandolow, T. (1991) 'The Moral Responsibility of Universities', in D. L. Thomson (ed.), *Moral Values and Higher Education,* New York: Suny Press.

Schopenhauer, A. (1999) *Prize Essay On the Freedom of the Will,* Cambridge: Cambridge University Press. First published 1839.

Smith, M. (2001) 'Education for Democracy', available online at http://www.infed.org/biblio/b-dem (accessed August 2006).

Straughan, R. (1989) *Beliefs, Behaviour and Education,* London: Cassell Education.

—— (1982) *Can We Teach Children to Be Good?* Milton Keynes: Open University Press.

Strawson, F. (1974) *Freedom and Resentment,* London: Methuen.

Warnock, G. J. (1971) *The Object of Morality,* London: Methuen.

Wilcox, J. R. and Ebbs, S. L. (1992) 'The Leadership Compass: Values and Ethics in Higher Education', ASHE-ERIC Higher Education Rep. No. 1.

Wilson, J. (1990) *A New Introduction to Moral Education,* London: Cassell Education.

Winch, C. and Gingell, J. (1999) 'Key Concepts in the Philosophy of Education', *International Review of Education,* 46 (3–4): 351–2.

Chapter 7

Community Involvement

Gary Taylor, Liam Mellor and Lizzie Walton

We can learn a great deal about our society and our rights and responsibilities as citizens through involvement in community projects. Although it might be beneficial to citizenship to find ways to improve our sense of belonging to society or the nation as a whole, projects that take place in the local community can often introduce citizens to the modern political process and show us the relevance of politics to our daily lives. We can be active citizens by taking an interest in issues in our local community and engaging with others to manage and improve the facilities we use. These activities could include such things as helping to run a youth group, fund-raising for the local school or participating in the design and maintenance of a community garden. Students can and do play an active role in their communities. They have numerous skills that can be passed on to others, and they, in turn, can learn from other members of the community. The spread of work-based learning in particular has provided many opportunities for students to gain academic credit for working in the community. It is also important to recognise that universities can cater to different groups within the community, and, by accommodating different points of view, they can enhance the learning experience of all students. Widening participation programmes in particular call upon universities to recognise their responsibilities towards the local community. When we talk about community involvement, therefore, we should be aware that it could include university and student activities in the community and community participation in the life of the university.

Higher Education and the Community

In addressing the issue of community involvement, we should begin by considering the relationship between universities and the community. We should recognise at the outset that universities operate in a variety of communities. They are usually located in geographic communities and function in a variety of virtual communities and communities of interest. It could be argued that what makes universities distinctive is their separation from the local community. This view of the university sees the pursuit of higher education in terms of a retreat from the life of the community. Alternatively, the university could be seen as an integral part of the community. This view might look for ways in which universities can cater for diverse needs within the community. It is this latter view that underpins the current chapter, and it is argued herein that universities and academics should regard themselves as part of wider communities, defined according to geographical location, shared interests and possibly shared spheres of influence. Academics already plug into communities. Our own academic disciplines are built upon scholarly endeavours in the past and the present. Our activities in terms of teaching and research will in turn make a contribution (however small) to the discipline and to the abilities and predispositions of our graduates who leave university armed with specialist knowledge and refined analytical skills. Many academics also draw their subject matter from the community. In the social sciences, we study communities and perhaps attempt to influence their future development. It could be argued indeed that academics who seek to divorce themselves from the community deprive themselves (and their students) of a sense of perspective to deal with important social issues and to exert influence upon society.

In order to appreciate the social role and responsibilities of the higher-education sector, it might be useful to be acquainted with the notion of the civic university. According to Barnett (2007: 33), a civic university is 'conscious of its responsibilities towards society and fulfilling a "public service" role is a way of acting out those responsibilities'. These responsibilities could be direct and immediate, such as assisting in the regeneration of a neighbourhood by offering the community access to university facilities for meetings or by actively engaging in research and funding bids directly related to the welfare of the local community. There are also long-term activities such as building sustainable partnerships with key stakeholders within the community. Whether immediate or long-term, such activities can have a dramatic impact upon the relationship between the university and the community. Zlotkowski (2007: 40) argues in favour of increased engagement between universities and the community. In his view, it is important to embrace the 'scholarship of engagement' in which universities and academics address and look for solutions to social problems. We should avoid, however, seeing this relationship purely in terms of what the university can do for the community. Boland and McIlrath (2007: 84) point out that if academics and universities are to engage with the community this must involve 'mutual listening, reciprocity and dialogue which is focussed on something beyond the self'. This is said to involve accommodating different views and 'strenuous, thoughtful, argumentative interaction with the wider world' (Boland and McIlrath 2007: 85). This would tend to suggest that a civic university must be dynamic and willing to adapt its activities to the needs and aspirations of the communities they serve.

A university can, of course, be a place where academics pursue personal-research agendas regardless of social value. It is clearly not essential for the academic system to respond to immediate social problems at the expense of all other work. Academics may well feel that they have a responsibility towards their discipline (and careers) that outweighs any transient social problem. This does not necessarily mean that we are without broader responsibilities. Barnett argues that academics should aim to promote the public good and that academics in general and those active in research in particular should 'understand that they have responsibilities towards the wider community' (2007: 32). Academics could, of course, determine what these responsibilities are and the importance they have when setting priorities for the academic year. It does, however, make sense for academics to consider (even if only from time to time) their place in the community and how their work can reach those beyond their lecture theatres. For some authors, it is important that we constantly respond and adapt to the needs of the community. Boland and McIlrath (2007: 83), for example, claim that we should be willing to adapt the philosophy and innovations we make in teaching and research 'to reflect and serve local culture, context and conceptions'. This includes adapting the products we create to 'non-native environments' (Boland and McIlrath 2007: 83). Engaging with the community can help academics see their teaching and their research in different contexts and, in turn, expand the opportunities open to us all.

The relationships between universities and the community are also influenced considerably by the behaviour and reputation of students in the local community. It is sometimes the case that students have a bad reputation, and a number of universities have taken steps to curb potentially disruptive student behaviour within local communities. This has been done in an attempt to improve relations between the university and the community and to protect the reputation of the university. Southampton University, for example, has developed an initiative whereby students are provided with a subsidised night bus to return them to campus at weekends. Leeds University has appointed a community liaison officer to deal with students in private accommodation in the large student-populated area of Headingley. David Attwood, Community Liaison Officer at Oxford Brookes University, claims that educating students 'about acceptable behaviour is part of our policy of being socially responsible to the community we serve' (cited in Chaudhuri 2000: 14). Research has shown that local residents are often concerned about increasing numbers of students in their neighbourhoods. Increased student presence is often accompanied by problems associated with late-night music and higher insurance premiums, the latter because students are often targeted in burglaries. It has been shown, however, that the presence of students can also help to increase house prices, maintain public transport in the area and, as graduates remain in the towns and cities where they went to university, contribute to the long-term development of an area (MacLeod and Ward 2006). Whilst universities and residents in university towns and cities might share an interest in curbing anti-social behaviour amongst pockets of the student population, it is evident that the presence of students per se should not be a cause of alarm for the local community. It could be argued that students and their universities accepting that they have responsibilities towards other members of the community could help to tackle disruptive behaviour.

There seem to be clear benefits to making links between universities and the business sector. Charles Clarke (2003), Secretary of Education under the Labour Government, points out that higher education needs to equip people with relevant skills and keep abreast with changes in the economy and society. He believes it is important for universities to strengthen their links with the business sector and that businesses should be invited to participate and contribute towards shaping the education offered by universities. Stephen Court (1997), a researcher with the Association of University Teachers, claimed that there are a number of benefits that can be derived from establishing partnerships with local and regional businesses. It is argued that universities can help to create jobs, provide valuable research and consultancy, as well as design and deliver training packages for local businesses. Court has also argued, however, that problems can arise from forging links with the business sector, especially where universities are perceived as subservient to the interests of business. In Court's view, teaching and research could suffer as a result of over-zealous attempts by universities to make themselves useful to the community. In his view, universities must 'defend their freedom to provide non-vocational courses and carry out research, as well as meeting local needs. A lot of work needs to be done on setting clear goals which are of benefit to universities as well as their communities' (Court 1997: 3). Here is a clear indication and warning that although the functions of universities can be enriched by fruitful partnerships with the community, it is important to make sure that universities are not relegated to a supporting role. Universities have their own part to play in the life of the community. There is certainly no need to defer to the business sector.

Universities can be significant in helping to regenerate local communities. Sir Howard Newby, the chief executive of the Higher Education Funding Council for England (HEFCE), claims that institutes of higher education should have a role in the development of economic competitiveness and social inclusion. He claims higher education now has a range of client groups 'not only students and their parents, but employers, regions, local communities, public services, and a host of other groups that we must now consider stakeholders' (Newby 2005: 10). Coventry University, for example, recognises the importance of helping to regenerate the local community and respond to local needs. When the car-building industry hit upon hard times in the neighbouring area of Ryton, Professor Ian Marshall (the Associate Pro-Vice Chancellor at Coventry University) said that he believed that the role of the university was in part to support the local community and that it should provide workers with the opportunity to update skills or enter other forms of employment. Marshall suggested that as part of 'our responsibility to our local community, we have the resources to support regeneration beyond just providing training. This is surely one of the main responsibilities of any modern university to its region and community' (Marshall 2006: 10). Herein lies a clear example of how universities, in recognising their broader civic roles, can assist the local area without sacrificing their distinctive character.

Involving Students in the Community: The Value of Work-Based Learning

One of the key ways to encourage student participation in the community is by allowing room in the curriculum for work-based learning or service learning, through which students spend part of their time working in the community. At Sheffield Hallam University, work-based learning has featured in a range of disciplines for over a decade (see Midgley 1998). In the social sciences, work-based learning has been offered for a number of years as an option for second- and third-year students. In many cases, students have chosen to work in community groups or through the university's own organisation, Hallam Volunteering. The success of these modules in encouraging students to reappraise their own roles in the community has been discussed elsewhere (see Taylor et al. 2006) and the recent introduction of a mandatory work-based-learning module for all second-year social-science students at Sheffield Hallam University provides opportunities for a greater number of students to engage with the community.

Work-based learning is challenging for students (and indeed for staff) on a number of levels. Boland and McIlrath (2007), for example, point out that students need to develop their abilities to apply the theory they learn in lectures and seminars and be able to reflect on their experiences of work. This involves a number of different skills including:

- knowing (understanding the subjects they study);
- doing (engaging with work);
- communicating (engaging with others).

In their view, it is important to work towards the integration of all three 'with a view to developing a sense of the civic self and a confidence in the potential for individual and collective engagement' (Boland and McIlrath 2007: 85). Having experience of work in the community can be rewarding and educative. It can also give the student's final degree a different dimension. Academics have expressed concerns about graduates who leave university without a thought for the community. David Donnison, from the Department of Urban Studies at the University of Glasgow, has argued that 'if students graduating from medical schools, law schools, planning schools and other parts of the university go forth to practice their professions without a thought for the communities in which they work- we shall have failed twice over!' (Donnison 2006: 48). Work-based learning in the community can be of benefit to a range of disciplines, and its relevance stretches far beyond a social-science curriculum.

Students are often provided with a range of opportunities to participate in the community through taking part in voluntary work. This work can be undertaken as part of a work-based-learning module or as an extra-curricular activity. Amber Cowan (2005) points out that students often find volunteering in community projects has a beneficial impact upon their physical and mental health. In particular, the feeling of being involved in something worthwhile can have a considerable effect upon the way we view our communities and ourselves. Taking part in community projects might also be seen as a form of political activity. Research conducted in the USA has found that young people sometimes see themselves as 'activist volunteers' and believe that voluntary action can lead to social and political change (Lopez et al. 2006). Although young people in the USA reject the view that civic service should be compulsory for high-school students, the majority of the 1,500 students interviewed believed that young people should be given the opportunity to participate in community service and, in so doing, earn money towards the costs of college (Lopez 2006). There is always the danger that making voluntary work 'compulsory' will undermine the altruism that lies behind at least some voluntary activity. This might be something that reduces the benefits of mandatory work-based-learning modules.

Universities have become increasingly involved in the development of modules on work-based learning, partly to further their own employability agendas. In the context of increased student fees and competition between universities, work-based learning is an attractive feature of many degree schemes. Charles Clarke (2003) argues that work-experience modules benefit both students and their employers. Students are thought to benefit because they have the opportunity to rehearse the role of the employee and to develop a firmer sense of their interests and career prospects. Students also gain valuable insights into living and working in the community and tend to become more active citizens. Research has shown that employers look upon participation in work-experience modules at universities favourably and that such modules have helped to improve the employment prospects of marginalised groups (see Universities UK 2002). Businesses are also thought to benefit because they can nurture new talent and influence the design of the education provided by the university sector. In so doing, the business sector can exert influence upon universities to provide an education suited to the needs of the contemporary economic system (Clarke 2003). Whilst recognising the importance of employability, we should avoid taking a too limited view of what this entails. Employability is not simply about equipping students with the skills necessary for the contemporary job market but also involves encouraging students to see themselves in a broader social context and asking them to reflect upon what they have to offer both employers and the community. This is certainly something we need to take into account when devising work-based-learning modules.

It is also important that work-based learning or service learning takes place as part of a reciprocal relationship with employers and organisations in the community. Whitney et al. (2007: 186) argue that service learning is a 'relational process' in which academics, community organisations and students are 'engaged in relationships not only of reciprocity, in which all contribute and all benefit, but of mutual learning, growth, and change'. It is understood that we must be open and willing to learn from each other. Kari and Skelton (2007) draw attention to the work carried out at the Jane Addams School for Democracy in Minnesota. Formed in 1996, the school aims to provide democratic education for new arrivals to the USA. They argue that students and academics often regard service learning as an opportunity to give something back to their community and that this approach is far too 'one-directional'. In their view, it is important to build relationships and to establish 'give and take partnerships' in which we all see ourselves as participants in a diverse community of learners. If we do indeed seek to establish sustainable relationships with groups in the community, this will surely have implications for teaching and learning. In looking for ways to arrange and coordinate service or work-based learning, Boland and McIlrath (2007) distinguish between transactional and transformative pedagogies of engagement. In the transactional pedagogy of engagement, the community is seen as a recipient of inputs from students. This can be problematic for once the student input is withdrawn the community is often no better off.

Under transformative pedagogies of engagement, greater credence is given to the development of a reciprocal relationship between academics, students and the community. They argue that it is important to understand the motives and values of those involved in the partnership as 'failure to respond to issues of local conception, culture and context may further marginalise pedagogies for civic engagement' (Boland and McIlrath 2007: 86–7). Work-based learning, indeed, is not simply a matter of sending students out into the community to 'do good'. It is about establishing dialogue with members of the community and responding to needs as they present themselves. In so doing, students can learn more about the work process and about their communities than by simply performing a predetermined function in return for academic credits.

Attracting Diverse Sections of the Community

So far, we have looked at community involvement in terms of the relationship between the university and the community and in the context of work-based learning. Community involvement can also be viewed according to the ways in which universities attract diverse sections of the community. Access to higher education is seen by some as one of the key ways to tackle social exclusion and to improve the prospects of marginalised sections of the community. Ken Livingstone, for example, has argued that higher education can be 'the biggest chance an individual has of escaping disadvantage and discrimination, and realising their potential for their own – and society's – benefit' (cited in Smithers 2004: 13). Tom Schuller (2002) suggests that higher education provides a way to involve people in networks and, in turn, to help people play a greater part in the life of their community. Stuart (2002) likewise argues that widening participation strategies in particular should help to provide marginalised groups with the ability and confidence necessary to participate in and lead projects to bring about social change. Attracting diverse sections of the community to higher education is not simply about increasing the number of students in the system. Managed effectively, an expanded higher-education system can help to transform who leads our communities. Higher education would seem to be particularly important in empowering communities to identify (and to find solutions to) the problems they face.

We should acknowledge that universities are still seen by some as the home of the talented few and that if universities are to attract a broader array of students, attempts must be made to dismantle barriers to studying at degree level. Many universities have attempted to draw in diverse sections of the community. Sheffield Hallam University has been particularly active in boosting the aspirations of local children by offering visits to universities for children and their parents at an early age (Weatherald and Layer 1998). Taster courses are sometimes offered in the hope of arousing interest in higher education. It is often the case that barriers to higher education can be reduced if universities are willing to adapt to the needs of their local communities and offer courses that are relevant to the needs of local people. The Penderry Project, coordinated by the adult-education centre at Swansea University, involved local residents' groups in planning non-credit-bearing modules and articulating their learning needs. These modules were run in local community centres rather than at the local university. This was one of the things that helped local people feel that they had ownership of their learning. It was found that approaching higher education in this way helped participants recognise possibilities in their community and improved their understanding of their own rights and power. It was pointed out, however, that 'such initiatives should be guided by realistic considerations of increasing empowerment. Those who are socially excluded are not just economically deprived and impoverished, they are also denied full citizenship rights' (Trotman and Pudner 1998: 54). When trying to reach the poorer sections of the community, universities must recognise that they need to offer something of value rather than expect those who have little or no experience of higher education to adopt some of the more traditional values circulating in the university sector.

Some important work is taking place to attract a greater number of black and ethnic-minority students into higher education. Tessa Blackstone (2004), Vice Chancellor at the University of Greenwich, has written in support of increasing the participation of black and ethnic-minority students in the belief that higher education can help to reduce social exclusion. In addition to benefiting the individuals concerned, she believes that these graduates will in turn provide role models for future generations. The University of Greenwich uses existing students as mentors for black and ethnic-minority school pupils in the local area in the hope of encouraging at least some of these pupils into higher education (see Blackstone 2004). This illustrates, amongst other things, how student participation in outreach work can in turn influence the character and composition of the university. Students can act as ambassadors of higher education and do a great deal to address and reduce at least some of the divisions between the university and the community.

Implications for Learning and Teaching

As we have seen, involving universities and students in the life of the community should not be viewed as a one-way process. If we strive to energise universities by adopting broader civic goals, this will have a significant impact upon the value we attribute to teaching. Zlotkowski (2007) claims that a scholarship of engagement allows for teaching itself to be seen as a 'form of scholarship' and that it recognises that universities should be concerned with the production and dissemination of socially useful knowledge. He points out that universities should not regard themselves as independent and unresponsive to social needs and that such arrogance rests upon the assumption that 'real knowledge is independent of affect and value judgements' (Zlotkowski 2007: 41). Ahmed Bawa (2007) has argued that we should acknowledge and be aware of the value of knowledge derived from engaging with the community and see this knowledge and engagement in the context of the production of knowledge. Without this, he believes that it is 'highly unlikely that it will expand beyond pilot experimentation' (Bawa 2007: 59). Community involvement entails entering into a series of reciprocal partnerships through which we learn as well as teach.

This approach to community involvement (and to learning and teaching) certainly has implications for the way we view citizenship. Welch (2007: 103) argues that universities should have an important role in helping students develop as citizens. This does not mean, however, that citizenship has to be taught in a traditional way. Ronald Barnett (2007), Professor of Higher Education at the University of London, provides some interesting advice on teaching citizenship. He claims that citizenship should be infused into the curriculum as a whole. Rather than teach specific modules on citizenship, he argues that we should be encouraged to recognise our connections with each other and with society as a whole. He believes that students should be encouraged to gain an appreciation of diverse views of the world and to 'develop a heightened sense of the other' (Barnett 2007: 32). A developed appreciation of citizenship involves seeing ourselves within a broader social and/or communal context. Roholt and Smyth (2007), for example, argue that citizenship is 'a process' and we 'accomplish citizenship by joining together to solve community problems (through either formal or informal politics) in ways that respect and support a shared future and result in creating something of lasting value for everyone' (2007: 157). It is clear that citizenship is something that we learn by doing and that the community provides us all with an arena to develop as citizens.

Conclusion

There are many ways that students and universities can be involved in their communities. Whether students go out into the community or the community makes use of the university, there are benefits to both the university and the community from nurturing sustainable partnerships. Closer ties with local schools and further-education colleges can help universities make contact with local people. Students can help to build relationships by working in the community, especially when they approach this work in a cooperative manner and show that they are willing to learn. Through involvement in their communities, students can learn at first hand what it is to be an active citizen. They can learn about decision-making, working with others, power structures, the problems of gaining funds for community projects and a range of other things by stepping out of the lecture theatre into the cut and thrust of community politics. By reassessing the relationship between the university and the community, by making use of work-based or service learning and by promoting a diversity agenda within universities, we might, in some small way, assist in the development of graduates who are aware of their connections with other people and who are willing to take an active part in the life and politics of their communities.

References

Barnett, R. (2007) 'Recovering the Civic University', in L. McIlrath and I. M. Labhrainn (eds), *Higher Education and Civic Engagement: International Perspectives,* Ashgate: Aldershot, pp. 25–36.

Bawa, C. C. (2007) 'Rethinking the Place of Community-Based Engagement at Universities' in L. McIlrath and I. M. Labhrainn (eds), *Higher Education and Civic Engagement: International Perspectives,* Ashgate: Aldershot, pp. 55–64.

Berliner, W. (2002) 'Clearing 2002: In the mix', *The Guardian,* 15 August, p. 16.

Blackstone, T. (2004) 'Education: Higher: Exclusion Zone', *The Guardian,* 26 October, p. 18.

Boland, J. and McIlrath, L. (2007) 'The Process of Localising Pedagogies for Civic Engagement in Ireland: The Significance of Conceptions, Culture and Context' in L. McIlrath and I. M. Labhrainn (eds),

Higher Education and Civic Engagement: International Perspectives, Ashgate: Aldershot, pp. 83–99.

Brown, R. (2002) 'Education: Higher: Opinion', *The Guardian,* 5 February, p. 14.

Chaudhary, V. (1998) 'On Campus: Consuming Passions', *The Guardian,* 31 March, p. 5.

Chaudhuri, A. (2000) 'Higher Education: A Real Headache', *The Guardian,* 31 October, p. 14.

Clarke, C. (2003) *The Future of Higher Education,* London: The Stationary Office.

Court, S. (1997) 'Opinion: Perils of Being Useful', *The Guardian,* 7 July, p. 3.

Cowan, A. (2005) 'Goodwill Can Go a Long Way', *The Times,* 26 November, p. 19.

Donnison, D. (2006) 'Public: Lest We Forget: Democracy, Neighbourhoods and Government', *The Guardian,* 2 November, p. 48.

Kari, N. and Skelton, N. (2007) 'Place Matters: Partnerships for Civic Learning' in L. McIlrath and I. M. Labhrainn (eds), *Higher Education and Civic Engagement: International Perspectives,* Ashgate: Aldershot, pp. 171–84.

Kingston, P. Q. (2002) 'Further Education: Is Adult Learning at Risk?' *The Guardian,* 17 December, p. 25.

Labhrainn, I. M. and McIlrath, L. (2007) 'Introduction' in L. McIlrath and I. M. Labhrainn (eds), *Higher Education and Civic Engagement: International Perspectives,* Ashgate: Aldershot, pp. xxi–xxvi.

Lopez, M. (2006) 'Youth Attitudes Towards Civic Education and Community Service Requirements', available online at http://www.civicyouth.org/PopUps/FactSheets/FS_Youth_Attitudes_Civic_Education.pdf (accessed 8 October 2007).

Lopez, M., Levine, P., Both, D., Keisa, A., Kirby, E. and Marcello, K. (2006) 'The 2006 Civic and Political Health of the Nation', available online at http://www.civicyouth.org/PopUps/2006_CPHS_Report_update.pdf (accessed 8 October 2007).

McIlrath, L. and Labhrainn, I. M. (2007) (eds) *Higher Education and Civic Engagement: International Perspectives,* Ashgate: Aldershot.

McKellar, Q. (2006) 'Tuition Fees Have to Happen for Vets', *The Daily Telegraph,* 5 July, p. 26.

MacLeod, D. and Ward, D. (2006) 'Doner Your Way', *The Guardian,* Education section, 24 January, p. 10.

Marshall, I. (2006) 'Comment: Peugeot Quits, but Universities Are There for the Long Haul', Education section, *The Guardian,* 25 April, p. 10.

Midgley, S. (1998) 'Flair in the Community', *The Guardian,* 7 July, p. 5.

Newby, H. (2005) 'Comment: Only Connect: The Message for the New Academic Year', Education section, *The Guardian,* 20 September, p. 10.

Preece, J. (1998) 'Introduction' in J. Preece, C. Weatherald and M. Woodrow (eds), *Beyond the Boundaries,* Leicester: NIACE, pp. 1–8.

Roholt, R. V. and Smyth, P. (2007) 'Civic Youth Work and Implications for Service Learning: Lessons from Northern Ireland' in L. McIlrath and I. M. Labhrainn (eds), *Higher Education and Civic Engagement: International Perspectives,* Ashgate: Aldershot, pp. 155–70.

Schuller, T. (2002) 'Opinion: Expanding Higher Education Is a Laudable Target, but We Must Not Forget That It Is Important for Those over 30, Too', Education section, *The Guardian,* 14 May, p. 13.

Smithers, R. (2004) 'Livingstone Risks Labour Ire to Attack Tuition Fees', *The Guardian,* 23 September, p. 13.

Stuart, M. (2002) *Collaborating for Change?* Leicester: NIACE.

Taylor, G., Todd, M., McManus, M., Long, J., McCarter, R., Digman, A. (2006) *The Impact of Work-Based Learning on Students' Understanding of Citizenship and their Role in the Community,* Southampton: SWAP.

Trotman, C. and Pudner, H. (1998) 'What's the Point' in J. Preece, C. Weatherald and M. Woodrow (eds), *Beyond the Boundaries,* Leicester: NIACE, pp. 47–55.

Universities UK (2002) *Enhancing Employability, Recognising Diversity,* London: Universities UK.

Weatherald, C. and Layer, G. (1998) 'As Broad as It's Long', in J. Preece, C. Weatherald and M. Woodrow (eds), *Beyond the Boundaries,* Leicester: NIACE, pp. 56–64.

Welch, M. (2007) 'Identifying and Teaching Civic Engagement Skills through Service Learning', in L. McIlrath and I. M. Labhrainn (eds), *Higher Education and Civic Engagement: International Perspectives,* Ashgate: Aldershot, pp. 103–20.

Whitney, B., McClure, J., Respet, A. and Clayton (2007) 'Service Learning as a Shared Developmental Journey: Tapping the Potential of the

Pedagogy' in L. McIlrath and I. M. Labhrainn (eds), *Higher Education and Civic Engagement: International Perspectives,* Ashgate: Aldershot, pp. 185–96.

Zlotkowski, E. (2007) 'The Case for Service Learning' in L. McIlrath and I. M. Labhrainn (eds), *Higher Education and Civic Engagement: International Perspectives,* Ashgate: Aldershot, pp. 37–52.

Chapter 8

Political Literacy

Hugh Bochel

Although, as noted elsewhere, the Crick Report (1998: 11) identified three main areas for 'effective education for citizenship' – social and moral responsibility, community involvement and political literacy – there is considerable overlap between concerns with 'political literacy' and concerns with 'active citizenship', and, indeed, for many people there is little or no distinction to be made between the two. This chapter therefore inevitably draws upon ideas and debates from the wider agenda, although it seeks to place these in the context of 'political literacy' as defined in the Crick Report (1998: 13):

> learning about and how to make themselves effective in public life through knowledge, skills and values . . . The term 'public life' is used in its broadest sense to encompass realistic knowledge of and preparation for conflict resolution and decision-making related to the main economic and social problems of the day . . . Such preparations are needed whether these problems occur in locally, nationally or internationally concerned organisations or at any level of society from formal political institutions to informal groups, both at local or national level.

'Political literacy' is therefore not simply concerned with describing or even analysing political institutions and government but is about being able to have an input and being able to exercise rights and responsibilities.

Concerns around political literacy are not new and have arguably been expressed periodically for over a century. For example, during the 1960s, 1970s and 1980s, 'research reported "low" levels of interest about contemporary political and economic problems among school students' (Frazer 1999: 6), and there were debates about whether schools should be teaching about 'political issues'; and in Scotland a secondary qualification, 'Higher' Modern Studies, which contained elements of such subject matter, emerged during the 1960s and 1970s. Yet, little progress was made (see Davies 1999 for a discussion of developments and initiatives in England), perhaps in part because of concerns around what teaching politics might involve, with many, particularly on the right, fearing that left-wing teachers would seek to influence pupils, and others, often on the left, fearing that it would simply reinforce the status quo; and because the neo-liberal influenced Conservative governments of the 1980s and 1990s were perhaps unlikely to trust teachers in the public sector to deliver such teaching, with, for example, the 1986 Education (No. 2) Act 'forbidding political activity in schools and requiring teachers in secondary schools to ensure that there was always a balanced presentation of opposing views' (Davies 1999: 130).

However, recent years have seen a renewed concern about political literacy, in conjunction with wider debates about citizenship, and these can be traced back to a number of factors including:

- concern over the perceived decline in levels of political engagement and political participation among young people, particularly as measured by turnout in elections;
- the ideas of social capital and human capital have encouraged some to consider ways in which the development of individuals and the contributions to society can be increased;

- concern over the level of familiarity of immigrants with 'the British way of life';
- the shift towards a more participative style of democracy.

One example of this is Pirie and Worcester (1998), who noted that what they termed the 'Millennial Generation' had little interest in politics (particularly party politics), or belief that voting in elections would make a difference, and low expectations of government, although they found that many were willing to take action on issues that concerned them. They suggest that we 'could be witnessing the emergence of an apolitical generation' (Pirie and Worcester 1998: 11). Others have made similar arguments, as outlined below.

Perhaps the most obvious initiative in relation to these concerns has been the introduction of citizenship into the National Curriculum for schools in England. However, there has been increasing interest in political literacy and associated ideas relating to students in higher education and also to those who are seeking to settle in the UK with the introduction of citizenship classes and tests.

However, it is primarily the political literacy of younger people, and initiatives mainly in schools and universities, which is the concern of the remainder of this chapter.

Evidence on Political Literacy

As noted above, educators' and politicians' interest in political literacy is not new, and, in 1978, the Hansard Society produced a report which called for the teaching of 'political education and political literacy' (Crick and Porter 1978). This, as noted by Davies (1999), received some support during the mid-1970s, but in the 1980s its position was eroded.

However, from the 1990s in particular there has been a renewed and widespread concern about the levels of political engagement and political participation among young people. One of the measures of this, which has been widely used, has been turnout in general elections, with successive elections from the 1990s showing low levels of turnout among the eighteen-to-twenty age group, consistently lower than other groups, with levels of turnout rising with each age category.

There has been other evidence to support the view that young people have become alienated or otherwise detached from political engagement, such as a Social and Community Planning Research survey for Barnardo's in 1996, which showed that only 21 per cent of young people said that they supported a political party, while 55 per cent said that they never read a newspaper (Roberts and Sachdev 1996). Similarly, a DEMOS report (Wilkinson and Mulgan 1995) also produced evidence of apparent ignorance and alienation among young people (although noting that on some issues young people felt strongly and were willing to participate, often through protest) and used this to argue for the teaching of civic education.

Even among the wider population, the Electoral Commission and Hansard Society's report, *An Audit of Political Engagement,* found that politics 'tends to be seen as something that is done by, and for, others' (2004: 10), and that interest in politics, political participation and political knowledge were relative low, arguing that 'Above all these findings suggest a need to re-build the relevance of "politics", both as a concept and as an activity worth taking part in' (Electoral Commission and Hansard Society 2004: 10). By the time of the fourth audit in 2007, the position had remained generally stable, although the report was able to claim that 'Public engagement is firmly on the political agenda' (Electoral Commission and Hansard Society 2007: 59) and, on the basis of relative stability since 2003, that 'If it is true that political engagement is not currently declining then there is some cause for optimism' (2007: 60).

However, it is possible to interpret much of this differently. For example, O'Toole et al. (2003) put forward three main criticisms of much research in this field:

1.   that much of the conception of what is 'politics' has been too narrow, having been imposed by researchers (and to some extent deriving from the use of quantitative survey

research methods) rather than allowing young people to express their own views;

2. a lack of participation in 'political' activities is then equated with non-participation in politics per se, with little exploration of what is happening in reality;

3. they suggest that most of the explanations for declining participation, such as cynicism about politicians, or lack of choice between parties apply equally to older age groups.

While it is possible to identify some potential flaws with these arguments, they do highlight some of the difficulties with much of the 'evidence' in this area. Their work in Birmingham, in which they used qualitative methods, intended to allow young people to respond in their own terms, suggested that for young people politics was about being able to express their views, but that they felt that there were considerable constraints upon their ability to do this. For these young people there was a view that, along with other lived experiences, such as class, gender and age, 'race' and racism were political issues, and 'that politics has become increasingly racialised; and that Britishness is a contested and contestable concept' (O'Toole et al. 2003: 354). In terms of young people's interaction with mainstream politics, O'Toole et al. reported that many respondents 'believed that they are excluded from, or marginalised within, mainstream politics because they are young [original emphasis]' (2003: 355). However, at the same time, there was a belief that young people and their concerns need to be represented. Yet, respondents reported that they were unlikely to vote in elections. As with other work, this suggests that young people may not participate in the formal political activities which are often studied, but perhaps the key message from this research, which contrasts with at least some other work, is that young people are far from politically apathetic but that they do feel marginalised or excluded, and that that they are not listened to.

In addition, not all research has supported the view that young people are politically apathetic. For example, a survey by Henn et al. (2005) showed that while they may have negative views of the world of politics, young people do show considerable interest in political affairs and are committed to the idea of elections and the democratic process, although they do not believe that the democratic process is open to them. Drawing upon the same research, Henn and Weinstein (2006) argue that:

> It is this very remoteness [of political parties and politicians] that adds to a sense that young people feel ignored and that they lack both political efficacy and any meaningful opportunities to influence those charged with governing on their behalf. If young people are to be reconnected to the political and democratic processes – and as part of this to be persuaded to vote in elections – then they need to feel confident that the political arena is an inclusive one, and that there are candidates worthy of their support and vote. The alienation that they currently claim to experience has roots that are deep and difficult to deracinate.

> (Henn and Weinstein 2006: 529)

Russell (2004: 353) has argued that the role of the media in highlighting the 'supposed disinterest' and 'apathy' of young people frequently legitimises the view that politics is not for the young and may mean that 'disengagement begets disengagement', calling upon academics, political parties and the media to ensure that they do not further widen the gap between electors and elected. On similar lines, Kimberlee (2002) suggests that such 'youth focused' explanations cannot on their own explain young people's apparent political indifference. He also argues that it is not enough simply to blame politicians and political structures for turning young people off politics, or to say that young people have different values which fall outside the ambit of the political parties. Instead, he suggests that rapid social changes may have impacted upon young people's journeys to 'adult status' so that they are different from their forebears, with previous 'certainties' such as work and family life and community and class cultures no longer ensuring an easy transition to citizenship.

Nevertheless, it is certainly the case that there is a strong view among significant segments of the media, politicians and educators that there has been 'a problem' in relations to levels of political literacy and engagement among young people, and that there has been a need to do something about it.

Responses to the Problem

Schools

The idea of teaching political literacy or political education has generally been an emotive one, with, for example, fears being expressed that children will be 'brainwashed' into either mindlessly accepting the status quo of society or of becoming equally mindless revolutionaries. It was only really with the 1997 Labour government that, with the exception of Modern Studies in Scotland, as discussed later, political literary, and citizenship, emerged onto the political agenda.

Given the concerns outlined above, the Government asked Bernard Crick to chair a group to produce a report to advise on citizenship education in schools. Notwithstanding the varied evidence on the extent of disengagement of young people, the resulting Crick Report (1998: 16) argued that things 'are inexcusably bad, and could and should be remedied'. The report included the statement that:

> We aim at no less than a change in the political culture of this country both nationally and locally: for people to think of themselves as active citizens, willing, able and equipped to have an influence in public life and with the critical capabilities to weigh evidence before speaking and acting; to build upon and to extend radically

to young people the best in existing traditions of community involvement and public service, and to make them confident in finding new forms of involvement and action among themselves. There are worrying levels of apathy, ignorance and cynicism about public life. These, unless tackled at every level, could well diminish the hoped-for benefits both of constitutional reform and of the changing nature of the welfare state. To quote from a speech by the Lord Chancellor earlier this year [1998] (on which we end this report): We should not, must not, dare note, be complacent about the health and future of British democracy. Unless we become a nation of engaged citizens, our democracy is not secure.

(Crick 1998: 7–8)

The report argued that 'the establishment of citizenship teaching in schools and community-centred learning and activities will bring benefits to pupils, teachers, schools and society at large' (Crick 1998: 9) including for pupils, empowering 'them to participate in society effectively as active, informed, critical and responsible citizens' (1998: 9) and for society in producing 'an active and politically-literate citizenry convinced that they can influence government and community affairs at all levels' (1998: 9).

The report also provided a consideration of what is meant by 'citizenship', recognising that this involves consideration of a variety of senses, drawing upon legal, moral and political arenas and including activities in the community, political engagement and respect for the rule of law. The report recommended the introduction of citizenship as a National Curriculum subject based upon three main strands: social and moral responsibility, community involvement and political literacy – 'Pupils learning about and how to make themselves effective in public life through knowledge, skills and values' (Crick 1998: 41). So, what is political literacy, and how is it being interpreted and operationalised? Crick and Porter (1978: 32) had previously argued that 'We see political literacy as more concerned with recognising accurately and accepting the existence of real political conflicts than with developing knowledge of the details of constitutional machinery.' However, as discussed later, it may be that this very emphasis upon the political has contributed to what appears to be the relatively slow implementation of this aspect of citizenship education.

In Scotland, as noted earlier, the introduction of Modern Studies as a qualification at 'higher' level came much earlier than Citizenship in England, and gradually spread across the secondary curriculum. Modern Studies ranges more widely than, for example, A-Level Politics and deals with domestic (Scottish and British) and international social and political issues. Writing in 1999, Maitles argued that 'Modern Studies is in many ways a success story', noting that 'Although it will be suggested that its influence in terms of institutional knowledge may be more limited than is generally thought, there is little doubt, especially at election times, that Modern Studies departments in schools contain many of the most politically literate students in the institution' (1999: 181). However, it is also the case that there remains a lack of evidence about the impact of Modern Studies in relation to concerns such as those considered by the Crick Report, including whether it affects levels of political literacy of those who study it compared with their peers in the education system. The importance of citizenship elsewhere in the curriculum has also been reinforced in Scotland, with responsible citizenship being one of the four purposes of A Curriculum for Excellence, although the approach differs from that in England as, rather than introducing a subject or area of citizenship in the curriculum, there is an expectation that other subjects should make their relevance to education for citizenship explicit.

In Northern Ireland and in Wales, the late 1990s also saw attention being paid to citizenship in schools, with the former adopting core values (pluralism, pursuit of social justice, acceptance of human rights and responsibilities and democracy) as underpinning educational policy (European Commission 2005), while, for the latter, personal and social education in schools includes 'empowering pupils to be active, informed and responsible citizens aware of their rights and committed to the practices of participative democracy and the challenges of being a citizen of Wales and the world' (Qualifications, Curriculum and Assessment Authority for Wales [QCAAW] 2000), with this becoming a statutory part of the curriculum from 2003.

Of course, it is worth noting that there is no consensus upon how citizenship and political literacy should be included in the curriculum, and some writers, such as Freire (for example 1985), have criticised the separation of 'political education' from other parts of the curriculum, arguing that to do so serves to misleadingly depoliticise the rest of the curriculum, whilst in reality all education is intrinsically political. Others, including Ofsted (2006) have suggested that it is best taught on its own.

Evidence on Progress

Given the emphasis upon citizenship, and political literacy as one element of it, in the National Curriculum in England, it is perhaps worth reflecting upon its impact so far.

In 2006, Ofsted produced a report, *Towards Consensus? On the Implementation of National Curriculum Citizenship in Secondary Schools in England*. The report suggested that while there had been significant progress in introducing citizenship, there remained a considerable gap, including, for example, a lack of specialist teachers and teaching. Where post-sixteen education in schools is concerned, the Ofsted report argued that whilst interest had been modest, a pilot programme had been successful in supporting 'critical democracy'. The Ofsted report chimed with other commentaries in recognising that there is no agreement on what 'citizenship' is, and suggested that for some schools this had been problematic, as they have emphasised their perceptions of the ethical and moral dimensions of citizenship, rather than the need to ensure that the subject 'is taught, learned, assessed and practised' (2006: 11). The National Curriculum outlines three strands of citizenship participation and responsible action – enquiry, communication and knowledge and understanding about becoming informed citizens – and while all relate to notions of political literacy, this is perhaps most true of the latter, where the reports suggested that 'schools need to give more thought to the issue of progression and revisiting content, so that knowledge and understanding are embedded' (Ofsted 2006: 16).

The Ofsted report also found that few schools had provided time for citizenship as a subject in its own right, often leading to cross-curricular work and 'an often uneasy and unsuccessful compromise' (2006: 23). Similarly, the frequent placing of a core of citizenship within PSHE (Personal, Social and Health Education) led to few programmes which were 'better than adequate' (Ofsted 2006: 24). On a more positive note, the report noted the dramatic rise in the number of pupils taking the GCSE short course on citizenship to more than 50,000 in 2006 (and that standards in citizenship were generally higher in those schools doing the GCSE than in those which were not).

The findings of the Ofsted report have been reflected by others. For example, from her study of secondary-school pupils, Chamberlin (2003: 96) suggested that 'the lack of knowledge, interest and involvement shown in most aspects of secondary education emphasises the magnitude of the task ahead'.

The National Foundation for Education Research (NFER) has undertaken a series of annual studies of citizenship education funded by the DfES (now the Department for Children, Schools and Families). Whilst these have to some extent reinforced conclusions and recommendations such as those in the Ofsted report, the 2007 report argued that there is also a need to help 'schools to overcome the structural challenges affecting citizenship delivery' (NFER 2007: 105), including a lack of status and visibility, pressure on curriculum time and competing policy priorities. Specifically on political literacy it suggested that it is 'an area of particular weakness due to teachers' lack of confidence in the subject matter and the fact it is perceived to be dry and difficult to teach' (NFER 2007: vi).

Perhaps one of the areas that has still not been adequately addressed, in attempts to deliver or ensure 'political literacy', is the balance between content and skills. Arguably, it is not specific knowledge or content that is important but the development of politically aware citizens, with the skills to think critically about the world. Without such skills then knowledge of institutions is likely to be of limited worth. It is also the case that many school students appear either to find citizenship boring or not even to recognise what it is, making it hard to disagree with Douglas, who argues that 'Political literacy has the potential to give citizenship its knowledge base and rigor' but emphasises the need to avoid both 'students and teachers resorting to a "politics is boring" statement' (2002: 1).

Higher Education

Debates around citizenship have also taken place within higher education, with the Dearing Report (1997) highlighting the importance of involvement with community and voluntary organisations for young people, while a report for HEFCE (Higher Eduation Funding Council for England) (Institute of Education 1996: 47) suggested that experience of higher education appears to make a distinctive contribution to increased tolerance of diversity, to commitment to equal opportunities and to resistance to political alienation. HEFCE's strategic plan for 2006–11 recognised that there is a role for universities in promoting citizenship. Clearly, citizenship is also firmly on the agenda within higher education, although the emphases tend to be upon active citizenship, participation and engagement, rather than on political literacy, with initiatives aimed at encouraging students to undertake volunteering becoming widespread in higher education.

That said, it is possible to identify some areas of higher education where political literacy has a higher profile, although, not surprisingly, these tend to be in areas where such an interest would be expected. It is therefore to be expected that the QAA benchmark statement for politics would state that:

> Politics is concerned with developing a
> knowledge and understanding of government

and society. The interaction of people, ideas and institutions provides the focus to understand how values are allocated and resources distributed at many levels, from the local through to the sectoral, national, regional and global. Thus analyses of who gets what, when, how, why and where are central, and pertain to related questions of power, justice, order, conflict, legitimacy, accountability, obligation, sovereignty, governance and decision-making.

(QAA 2007a: 3)

Or that for international relations it would contain similar sentiments but in an international context. Similarly, the benchmark statement for social policy and administration, while recognising the breadth of the subject, contains a number of topics which would clearly relate to political literacy (QAA 2007b).

Within higher education, the Fund for the Development of Teaching and Learning initiative, FDTL5, which was relevant for the politics discipline, has seen a number of projects relating to a greater or lesser extent to citizenship, including political literacy: Teaching Citizenship in Higher Education, The Scholarship of Engagement for Politics, Case Based Learning in Politics, PREPOL – Developing and Pre-entry and Initial Guidance Package for the Study of Politics and International Relations, and the ALAC – Active Learning, Active Citizenship – project from which this monograph has developed. These projects have all drawn upon ideas associated with the citizenship agenda, although, perhaps inevitably given that they have at least in part designed for consumption by politics students, whose levels of political literacy might be expected to be relatively high, most have perhaps tended to focus upon engagement rather than political literacy. The Centres for Excellence in Teaching and Learning initiative (CETL) also provided funding for CRUCIBLE (a 'centre of excellence in education in human rights, social justice and citizenship'), although again the emphasis is upon a broader scale and any concern with political literacy is likely to be relatively minor. In addition, the Higher Education Academy's subject centres for Social Policy and Social Work (SWAP) and for Sociology, Anthropology and Politics (C-SAP) have both supported smaller-scale projects relating to citizenship, of which a few have had clear links to political literacy for undergraduate students.

Overall, whilst initiatives in higher education have inevitably been less structured, and arguably less comprehensive, than in school-age education, concerns with active citizenship and political literacy can be seen to have emerged in a variety of forms. However, there is as yet much less evidence on their impact.

It may also be worth noting that some writers have made links between perceived changes within higher education and concerns with political literacy among young people. Macfarlane (2005), for example, brings together consideration of citizenship education for young people with what he calls the 'citizenship responsibilities of the academic community' (2005: 298), arguing that the latter has tended to be overlooked amid the concerns for the education of children and young adults. He claims that 'to be an academic citizen demands active interest in decision-making processes as a member of a University. Here, decision making takes place at different levels: the department, faculty (or school) and university level' (Macfarlane 2005: 301), but he suggests that hierarchy as tended to strengthen while collegiality has weakened and no longer balances it to the extent that it used to, and that the 'political literacy' of academic staff has been damaged by the decline of collegial decision-making and the rise of a management culture (although he also recognises the role of other factors, such as the casualisation of academic labour), so that 'In common with the disengagement thesis more generally within society, academic citizenship appears to be in a similar state of crisis and retreat' (Macfarlane 2005: 309). He suggests that a revitalised commitment to service is necessary if academic citizenship is to survive.

Other Initiatives

There have also been a number of other initiatives, both relating to and to some extent external to the education system. Within government, but outside the education system, perhaps the most obvious developments have been around active citizenship, and particularly volunteering, and in relation to the introduction of a 'Life in the UK' test for those who seek to become UK citizens or who wish to remain permanently in the country, some of the questions from which might be said to imply at least some minimal level of political literacy.

Outside government there have also been developments. For example, the Citizenship Foundation seeks to encourage and enable people to play an active role in democratic society. Its activities are focused in particular on young people, and it does this in a variety of ways, including not only its own activities but also providing a range of resources, some designed to support citizenship teaching in schools, but others effectively being freestanding. It includes political literacy as an important part of this, again with a number of resources available to support it.

The much older Hansard Society, whose primary aim is to promote parliamentary democracy, has also demonstrated a long-standing concern with political literacy, including the work of Crick and Porter (1978). It too has developed resources aimed at students and teachers of citizenship in schools but also has its own initiatives, including HeadsUp (www.headsup.org.uk), which provides a forum for young people to discuss political issues. It also undertakes research, on its own and jointly with other organisations, on issues associated with citizenship, including political literacy.

Finally, it is worth remembering that, while many of their peers may not be politically engaged, many young people are involved in volunteering and campaigning and that these activities can encourage the development of young people's political knowledge, awareness and understanding (for example, see Roker et al. 1999). There are also those students who study Politics at A Level, of whom there were more than 24,000 in 2007 . . .

Indeed, contrary to the evidence that young people are disinterested in politics, recent years have seen significant increases in the numbers taking A-Level politics and in the numbers applying for 'politics' courses at universities. There is, too, a further debate about the role, content and consequences of citizenship education or political education in a liberal democratic society (see, for example, Frazer 1999; Levinson 1999).

Conclusion

It is apparent from this chapter that while there may have been significant developments in relation to citizenship education, particularly within schools, but to some extent also within higher education, progress with the 'political literacy' element has been relatively slow. There may be a number of reasons for this, including the lack of specialist subject expertise among staff, the fact that teaching about 'politics' beyond basic institutional structures remains contentious for many, and the pressure upon the curriculum more generally, meaning that citizenship is often taught in combination with other subjects, particularly personal, social and health education (PSHE).

One of the strands that emerges from much of the work on citizenship, and political literacy in particular, is the need to achieve a balance between subject knowledge and discussion and analysis, with views being expressed that one of the reasons why young people lack interest in knowledge is that they do not understand it, but that teaching and learning focused upon political institutions, for example, can be dry and uninteresting; at the same time, while discussion and debate are needed to enliven such topics, they are not on their own sufficient, so they cannot take place in a knowledge vacuum. It is therefore important to retain the focus of political literacy on the overall aims of political literacy – embedding notions of conceptual knowledge and values, understanding of key institutions and actors and the ability to debate, argue and come to a considered view.

References

Chamberlin, R. (2003) 'Citizenship? Only If You Haven't Got a Life: Secondary School Pupils' Views of Citizenship Education', *Westminster Studies in Education,* 26 (2): 87–97.

Crick, B. and Porter, A. (1978) *Political Education and Political Literacy,* London, Longman.

Crick Report (1998) *Education for Citizenship and the Teaching of Democracy in Schools: Final Report of the Advisory Group on Citizenship,* London: Qualifications and Curriculum Authority (QCA).

Davies, I. (1999) 'What has Happened in the Teaching of Politics in Schools in England in the Last Three Decades and Why?', *Oxford Review of Education,* 25 (1–2): 125–40.

Dearing, R. (1997) *Report of the National Committee of Inquiry into Higher Education,* London: DfEE.

Douglas, A. (2002) 'Educating for Real and Hoped For Political Worlds: Ways Forward in Developing Political Literacy', available online at http://www.citized.info/?r_menu=res_art&strand=4 (accessed 7 September 2007).

Electoral Commission and Hansard Society (2004) *An Audit of Political Engagement,* London: The Electoral Commission and Hansard Society.

Electoral Commission and Hansard Society (2007) *An Audit of Political Engagement 4,* London: The Electoral Commission and Hansard Society.

European Commission (2005) *Citizenship Education at School in Europe: United Kingdom (England, Wales, Northern Ireland)*, Brussels: European Commission.

Frazer, E. (1999) 'Introduction: The Idea of Political Education', *Oxford Review of Education*, 25 (1–2): 5–22.

Freire, P. (1985) *The Politics of Education*, South Hadley, Mass.: Bergin and Garvey.

Henn, M., Weinstein, M. and Forrest, S. (2005) 'Uninterested Youth? Young People's Attitudes towards Party Politics in Britain', *Political Studies*, 53 (3): 556–78.

Henn, M. and Weinstein, M. (2006) 'Young People and Political (In)Activism: Why Don't Young People Vote?', *Policy and Politics*, 34 (3): 517–34.

Institute of Education (1996) *The Wider Benefits of Higher Education*, London: HEFCE.

Kimberlee, R. (2002) 'Why Don't British Young People Vote at General Elections?, *Journal of Youth Studies*, 5 (1): 85–98.

Levinson, M. (1999) 'Liberalism, Pluralism and Political Education: Paradox or Paradigm', *Oxford Review of Education*, 25 (1–2): 38–58.

Macfarlane, B. (2005) 'The Disengaged Academic: the Retreat from Citizenship', *Higher Education Quarterly*, 59 (4): 296–312.

Maitles, H. (1999) 'Political Education in Schools', *International Journal of Inclusive Education*, 3 (2): 181–90.

National Foundation for Education Research (2007) *Vision versus Pragmatism: Citizenship in the Secondary School Curriculum in England*, London, DfES.

Ofsted (2006) *Towards Consensus? Citizenship in Secondary Schools,* Manchester, Ofsted.

O'Toole, T., Marsh, D. and Jones, S. (2003) 'Political Literacy Cuts Both Ways: The Politics of Non-Participation among Young People', *The Political Quarterly,* 74 (3): 349–60.

Pirie, M. and Worcester, R. (1998) *The Millennial Generation,* London: Adam Smith Institute.

Qualifications, Curriculum and Assessment Authority for Wales (ACAAW) (2000) *Personal and Social Education Framework Key Stages 1 to 4,* Cardiff: QCAAW.

Qualifications Assessment Authority (QAA) (2007a) *Politics and International Relations: Subject Benchmark,* Mansfield, QAA.

QAA (2007b) *Social Policy and Administration: Subject Benchmark,* Mansfield, QAA.

Roberts, H. and Sachdev, D. (1996) *Young People's Social Attitudes: Having Their Say, the Views of 12–19 Year Olds,* London: Barnardo's.

Roker, D, Player, K. and Coleman, J. (1999) 'Young People's Voluntary and Campaigning Activities as Sources of Political Education', *Oxford Review of Education,* 25 (1–2): 185–98.

Russell, A. (2004) 'The Truth About Youth? Media Portrayals of Young People and Politics in Britain', *Journal of Public Affairs,* 4 (4): 347–54.

Wilkinson, H. and Mulgan, G. (1995) *Freedom's Children: Work, Relationships and Politics for 18–34 Year-Olds in Britain Today,* London: DEMOS.

Chapter 9

Conclusion

Hugh Bochel, Patrick Dillon, Karl Donert, Janet Kay,
Richard McCarter, Mike McManus and Gary Taylor

The conclusion to this monograph is written jointly by many of the authors who have contributed chapters. We recognised very early on that we would approach the issues from a variety of angles. This is partly because the authors contained herein come from different subject backgrounds and have throughout this project looked at active learning and active citizenship in a variety of ways. The monograph gave us the space to discuss each other's rationales and pedagogies and the opportunity to look more closely at the connections between active learning and active citizenship.

Despite the differences between the authors, it became increasingly apparent during the lifetime of the project on active learning and active citizenship (ALAC) that there were connections between our approaches but that these were sometimes obscured by our own subject backgrounds and the vocabulary we use and take for granted. It was tempting at times to refer to members of the team as either 'educationists' or 'politicos'. In meetings, by design or not, we would often sit on opposite sides of the table. The battle lines were drawn, and it made for a lively exchange of views. Is active learning more important than active citizenship? Should we concentrate more on process or content? Do we want to use active learning to produce something on active citizenship or is active citizenship merely the subject matter we use to explore the nature and potential of active learning? Gradually, members of the team began to identify connections, but were these merely fleeting coincidences or could they be developed into coherent arguments? In the desire to record at least some of the dialogue, the ALAC team embarked upon this monograph and agreed to write a collective conclusion. We knew that the conclusion could not be a summary of what each of us believes individually and that we would have to identify differences and look for common ground. This approach, and its foundation in teamwork and cooperation, generally reflects the progress of the ALAC project itself.

The conclusion was written in a number of stages. We began in February 2007 with a writers' workshop, facilitated by Professor Ranald MacDonald at Sheffield Hallam University. The purpose of this workshop was to explore the aims and possible structure of the monograph, but it was clear that each member of the ALAC team used it in part to glean some understanding of where his or her chapter (or particular interest) would sit in the project overall. In participating in the workshop and being open about our particular aims, we were able to see more clearly the differences and similarities between the approaches advanced by members of the group. In November 2007, we held a second one-day workshop to outline the conclusion. At this workshop, we divided into two groups (the educationists and the politicos) and attempted to explore the implications of our own approach for the apparent preoccupations of the other group. The 'educationists' were asked to consider the following question: 'How can active learning improve our understanding of citizenship?' The 'politicos' were asked to consider the issue from the opposite direction: 'In what ways can active citizenship be seen as a form of active learning?' The groups then came together to consider the relationship and connections between active learning and active citizenship. There were clearly limits to what we could achieve in one day, so the final stage in writing the conclusion involved one member of the group collating the notes from the day, making some additions and sending it to the next member of the team who likewise made additions, with this process continuing until each member of the team had the opportunity to add to the conclusion. What follows is the result of this process.

Active Learning

Where the discussion of active learning is concerned, the chapters reflect the more general ideas which have underpinned much of the work for the project and, at the same time, some of the more specific issues and concerns which have emerged in relation to seeking to relate active learning and active citizenship in the curriculum. For example, the chapter by McManus contains a number of definitions which are essentially contextual, that is, situations in which active learning might happen, for example, work-based or problem-based. In contrast, the definitions introduced by Foo et al. are largely instrumental, that is, characteristics of active learning. The chapter by Foo et al. is highly ALAC-specific, it is framed within its own definition of active learning, whereas the chapters by McManus and Dillon are at a high level of generality. All of the chapters are framed in particular views and philosophies of education – as Pring (2000) says education is 'essentially contestable', but these are not always explicit.

McCarter, on the other hand, has approached the subject matter and the theme of 'active' and activity. This chapter tries to understand what learning is when combined with technology and rich media by exploring the notions of what is meant by active learning and the use of media and the relationship between what an 'active' learner does and what an interactive piece of learning attempts to do. One is characterised by notions of participation, ownership, community, collaboration and reflection; the other tends to be associated with interaction with something or someone. The nature of the interaction might be with a set of activities in a multimedia learning package which are carefully coordinated to produce a set of outcomes or, alternatively, characterised by working actively as part of a group to achieve an objective. Whichever way the subject of active learning is explored, it appeals to educationists because the pedagogy is distancing itself from 'passive' modes of learning, which are often the case when learners are passively viewing rich media content or alternatively sitting motionless in a lecture theatre with no regard or thought to further outcomes. The chapter by McManus has a strong focus on work-based learning and, therefore, the theory sits within an experiential 'doing' approach to learning whereas the relationship with being 'active' and rich media content can be seen as combining the 'doing' with capturing real-life world events and making sense of these events through the medium of audio, animation or video. This is further characterised by the learner also being a producer of media and understanding what the 'doing' has achieved over a period of time and in many kinds of interactions rather than a singular one-off event.

Learning is empowerment – the ability to pursue rights and responsibilities, make choices and take actions; these in turn define citizenship. The relationships are not static because everything is constantly changing: the relationships between educational, economic and political systems are different today than they were in the 1960s.

The process model outlined in McManus – autonomy/activity, engagement, reflection – is evident in the construction and presentation of the content in the ALAC website. The site is not merely a collection of independent and disconnected resources. Its construction is underpinned by a pedagogy of active learning. It should also be noted that teaching strategies and models discussed in different chapters are more than just pedagogies; they also contain implicit philosophies. The French tradition of the memoir – an essay that synthesises one's interests and what one knows, but in a different situation (essentially a process of reflection) – and the 'capstone' notion in North America entail a summative reflective process. In the UK, we try to apply things in a new context. The initial parts of the model – activity and engagement – are formative parts of this reflective process. The journey (the process of becoming a citizen) is not linear or 'once only'. It is a cyclical and recurring activity.

Dillon's pedagogy of connection has two important components: (i) the contextualisation of learning and (ii) tools or strategies for facilitating learning. Learning through connection is consequential, transformative and active, with students progressively taking control of their own learning. McManus sees this happening through stages of activity, engagement and reflection. This is not a linear process; the stages are interdependent and interrelated. Being transformed is a liminal process where one's identity changes and roles are redefined (for example, teachers to facilitators). Asking students to change roles (for example, consumer to producer) leads to similar uncertainties; it takes them to the edge of their comfort zones (to the 'boundaries' in Dillon's terms). This begs the question of how one makes the boundary crossings, how one accommodates oneself to a new space – arguably part of the process of becoming autonomous. One may see the world differently as a result of the process, and one's potential to influence the situation and processes of behaviour and learning through which transformation is achieved. Each individual will engage with the principles and processes in different ways – the 'flexibility' which is central to McManus's account of active learning. We create clones rather than citizens if learning is not flexible; the process needs to reflect difference.

Donert considers that universities have perhaps taken for granted some of the basic competences needed to achieve student-centred active approaches and urges us to consider the importance of ICT literacy for active learning. We need such literacy to connect a highly complex, diverse, real world to high structured forms of learning. He talks about simulating the real world.

It is important also to reflect on the nature of the learners and the context they find themselves learning in. They are learning in their worlds, not ours. Hence the indispensable nature of technology as fundamental component of active learning. However as Donert comments this is only possible as long as a learning dialogue between learners takes place, assuming that tutors are also learners in the learning process.

Active Citizenship and the Political Process

The chapters on active citizenship also illustrate some of the definitional challenges associated with our ideas. For example, is an active citizen also, and necessarily, somebody who takes responsibility in society? If so, what kind of responsibilities would be considered as legitimate (and by whom)? It is arguably the case that a significant part of the reason for recent governments' emphasis upon active citizenship has been a perceived need to encourage citizens to take on greater responsibilities in society, with both Conservative and Labour governments since the early 1990s trying to involve citizens in the provision and shaping of services. In terms of how this has related to individuals, it has involved attempts to shift responsibility for their lives, for example, by providing for their own pension and taking greater responsibility for their own health; in addition, there have been a series of attempts to involve people in areas such as education, including through initiatives related to parental choice, and there have been restatements of the notions that 'rights' to services and to state support effectively go hand in hand with responsibilities, such as to work, where work is available, and perhaps to behave in line with perceived societal norms.

However, these policy developments and the ideas behind them also throw up some questions which are pertinent to ideas of active citizenship. For example, do people really want or need choice? Or are people primarily concerned with having good-quality public services which are responsive to their needs so that choice essentially only becomes more important when there are distinct problems with some of the options?

There are also potentially questions over how active citizenship, or at a minimum, some of the ideas generally associated with it, such as choice and participation of individuals, interact with and relate to different forms of government and politics? In attempting to address this question, we might need to take into account traditional representative democracy, more participative forms of decision-making and the responsibilities of individuals. There are a variety of ways in which individuals can be empowered or given influence and control over their own lives. In relation to representative democracy, active citizenship can sometimes be seen as helping to 're-engage' people with traditional forms of politics, as reflected in sections of the discussion of political literacy in Case Studies 5 and 6 on the ALAC site. From another perspective, active citizenship can be seen as relating to the empowerment of citizens in relation to themselves as individuals (for example, through attempts to increase 'choice') or though reducing the role of the State and thus increasing the responsibilities of the individual. Another view might stress empowerment in relation to decision-making by social and political institutions. Active citizenship and greater levels of involvement in decision-making can be seen to influence and even improve policies and to assist in removing at least some of the barriers to their successful implementation. On the other hand, active citizenship, associated with more participative approaches to democracy, might threaten some aspects of representative democracy, as policies made following active participation by (some) citizens might not accord with the values or wishes of our elected representatives. Yet, the notions of representative government and liberal democracy continue to be the mainstay of the UK's systems of government and politics. Therefore, there may need to be some consideration of what active citizenship really means for policy-making and for representative government.

Given the use of rich multimedia on the ALAC website it is worth raising the issue of the significance of IT as a promoter of democracy and an enabler of the active participation of citizens. To what extent should it be seen as a help or a hindrance? This point is recognised from all political standpoints. The question might be whether active engagement of many citizens could hinder the political process.

Active Learning and Political Understanding

At one level of generality, active citizenship and active learning involve similar dispositions to think and act in particular ways . Both combine activity with critical and analytical thinking and reflection: problems or issues are identified, and alternative courses of action considered. This might involve taking into account the views of others or a consideration of the possible response of different groups or individuals.

Conclusion

In discussing the issue of religious fundamentalism and political violence as in Case Study 5, for example, an active learner might consider what constitutes the problem, the nature of evidence that exists about the problem, who has produced the evidence, what kind of vested interests exist and so on. A passive learner might be willing simply to accept the diagnosis offered by another scholar or to dismiss the problem as of no direct, personal concern.

In terms of political understanding, accepting the 'received' views of dominant political actors is a form of passivity. Rather than accept a handed-down 'definitive' answer, the active learner is more likely to welcome diverse perspectives and be willing to think his or her way through alternatives. By working through these alternatives, he or she actively engages with the material, develops his or her own views and forms relevant and challenging questions. Relying primarily on easily accessible views, such as those of the main political parties, is passive. The active learner is more likely to seek out a wider range of views, extending beyond political parties and into the relevant communities, pressure groups and churches, and to identify the rationales underpinning these. In terms of policy responses, adopting a relatively simplistic approach to identifying possible 'solutions' is passive. An active learner is more likely to consider the wider implications that might arise from different approaches, such as considering the future relationship of religion to the state not only in the UK and Ireland, but perhaps also in the USA and the EU, as well as other possible economic and social outcomes.

By facing new challenges, we are involved in active learning. We do not (or should not) expect to have answers to enable us to navigate our way through change and uncertainty. Instead, we might expect some indication of the problems to be overcome and the resources (if any) at our disposal to deal with these problems. Being able to learn and to adapt to new circumstances can be a source of empowerment. Empowerment can come about through activity in our communities, and active learning can empower us to participate more fully.

Conclusion

This monograph and the chapters it contains make the case for links between activity and learning and activity and citizenship. It is argued that we need to make the link(s) between learning and citizenship (which is a broader educational issue). This in turn raises the question over whether active learning and active citizenship are things that higher education should embrace. And do we need to see these two forms of activity as distinct, or should we work towards developing a theoretical framework and approaches to teaching that includes each of the activities? Does engaging in active learning with a citizenship content change people's values and behaviour as citizens?

To be an active learner and an active citizen involves a commitment to the deconstruction and reconstruction of meaning. From a political point of view, this means that an active citizen is somebody who deconstructs his or her understanding of social and political worlds. This might be through active engagement in the political process or by actively scrutinising the political messages we receive. For the citizen, developing this understanding is a foundation for further activity. What we mean by activity is certainly not restricted to any prescribed form of political participation. Indeed, we suggest that activity should be viewed in terms of the reconstruction of meaning through engagement (whether personal or intellectual) with the political system. It could be argued indeed that we become active citizens as soon as we recognise that politics does have something to do with us, that we are members of numerous communities and that we have responsibilities towards each of these communities. From this point of view, an active citizen is somebody who is constantly involved in attempting to understand the politics of his or her communities and who shows some commitment to playing an active part in shaping how these communities develop. Active citizenship could be said to involve deconstructing the present to reconstruct the future.

References

Anscombe, G. E. M. (1958) 'Modern Moral Philosophy', *Philosophy,* 33: 38–40.

Carr, D. (1999) 'Cross Questions and Crooked Answers: Contemporary Problems for Moral Education', in J. Mark Halstead and T. H. McLaughlin (eds), *Education in Morality,* London: Routledge, pp. 24–44.

Cleaver, E., Ireland, E., Kerr, D. and Lopes, J. (2005) *Citizenship Education Longitudinal Study: Second Cross-Sectional Survey 2004. Listening to Young People: Citizenship Education in England (DfES Research Report 626),* London: DfES.

Colby, A., Ehrlich, T., Beaumont, E., and Stephens, J. (2003) 'Pedagogical Strategies for Educating Citizens', in A. Colby et al. (eds), *Educating Citizens: Preparing America's Undergraduates for Lives of Moral and Civic Responsibility,* San Francisco, Calif.: Jossey-Bass.

Citizenship Advisory Group (1998) *Education for Citizenship and the Teaching of Democracy in Schools: Final Report of the Advisory Group on Citizenship (the 'Crick' Report'),* London: Qualifications and Curriculum Authority.

Dewey, J. (1909) *Moral Principles in Education,* Boston, Mass.: Houghton Mifflin Company.

—— (1938) *Experience and Education,* New York: Collier Books.

Downie, R. S. (1964) 'Social Roles and Moral Responsibility', *Philosophy,* 39 (147): 29–36.

Eshelman, A. (2004) 'Moral Responsibility', *Stanford Encyclopedia of Philosophy,* available online at http://www.seop.leeds.ac.uk/entries/moral-responsibility. (Accessed December 2008.)

Farbo, M. (2006) 'Dare American Higher Education Build a New Social Order? In the Service of Whom and the Promotion of What in the Education', in B. Holland and J. Meeropol (eds), *A More Perfect Vision: The Future of Campus Engagement,* Providence, RI: Campus Compact. Available online at http://www.compact.org/20th/papers. (Accessed December 2008.)

Feinberg, J. (1968) 'Collective Responsibility', *Journal of Philosophy,* 65 (21): 222–51.

Harkavy, I. (2006) 'The Role of Universities in Advancing Citizenship and Social Justice in the 21st Century', *Education, Citizenship and Social Justice,* 1 (1): 5–37.

Hersch, R. H., Miller, J. P. and Fielding, G. D. (1980) *Models of Moral Education,* New York: Longman Inc.

Hersh, R. H. and Schneider, C. G. (2005) 'Fostering Personal and Social Responsibility on College and University Campuses', *Liberal Education.*

Holland, J. R. (1991) 'Moral Values in Higher Education', in D. L. Thomson (ed.), *Moral Values and Higher Education,* New York: Suny Press.

Honderich, T. (1988) *The Consequences of Determinism: A Theory of Determinism,* Vol. II, London: Clarendon.

Jonathan, R. (1999) 'Agency and Contingency in Moral Development and Education', in J. Mark Halstead and T. H. McLaughlin (eds), *Education in Morality,* London: Routledge, pp. 62–78.

Jones, R. and Thomas, L. (2005) 'The 2003 UK Government Higher Education White Paper: a Critical Assessment of Its Implications for the Success of the Widening Participation Agenda', *Journal of Education Policy,* 20 (5): 615–630.

Kohlberg, L. (1981) *The Philosophy of Moral Development: Moral Stages and the Idea of Justice,* New York: Harper & Row.

Kuh, G. (2005) 'Do Environments Matter? A Comparative Analysis of the Impress of Different Types of Colleges and Universities on Character', *Journal of College and Character,* available online at http://www.collegevalues.org/articles.cfm?a=1&id=239. (Accessed December 2008.)

McPhail (1982) *Social and Moral Education,* Oxford: Blackwell.

Nixon, J. (2004) 'Learning the Language of Deliberative Democracy', in M. Walker and J. Nixon (eds), *Reclaiming Universities from a Runaway World,* Buckingham: Open University Press, pp. 114–27.

Pyke, N. (2002) 'Citizenship: Critical Thinking Not Propaganda', *Independent,* 27 September.

Raillon, P. (1984) 'Alienation, Consequentialism and the Demands of Morality', *Philosophy and Public Affairs,* 13 (2): 134–71.

Sandolow, T. (1991) 'The Moral Responsibility of Universities', in D. L. Thomson (ed.), *Moral Values and Higher Education,* New York: Suny Press.

Schopenhauer, A. (1999) *Prize Essay On the Freedom of the Will,* Cambridge: Cambridge University Press. First published 1839.

Smith, M. (2001) 'Education for Democracy', available online at http://www.infed.org/biblio/b-dem (accessed August 2006).

Straughan, R. (1989) *Beliefs, Behaviour and Education,* London: Cassell Education.

—— (1982) *Can We Teach Children to Be Good?* Milton Keynes: Open University Press.

Strawson, F. (1974) *Freedom and Resentment,* London: Methuen.

Warnock, G. J. (1971) *The Object of Morality,* London: Methuen.

Wilcox, J. R. and Ebbs, S. L. (1992) 'The Leadership Compass: Values and Ethics in Higher Education', ASHE-ERIC Higher Education Report Number 1 Washington, DC: School of Education and Human Development, George Washington University.

Wilson, J. (1990) *A New Introduction to Moral Education,* London: Cassell Education.

Winch, C. and Gingell, J. (1999) 'Key Concepts in the Philosophy of Education', *International Review of Education,* 46 (3–4): 351–2.